EVERYDAY CHEAPSKATE'S
GREATEST TIPS

EVERYDAY CHEAPSKATE'S

Greatest Tips

500 SIMPLE STRATEGIES FOR SMART LIVING

BY MARY HUNT

RUNNING PRESS
PHILADELPHIA · LONDON

© 2005 by Mary Hunt

Printed in the United States

9   8   7   6   5   4   3   2   1

Digit on the right indicates the number of this printing

Library of Congress Control Number 2004097158

ISBN 0-7624-2335-8

Cover and interior designed by Matt Goodman
Edited by Greg Jones
Typography: Times New Roman and Helvetica

Everyday Cheapskate™ is a trademark owned by Mary Hunt.

This book may be ordered by mail from the publisher.
Please include $2.50 for postage and handling.
But try your bookstore first!

Running Press Book Publishers
125 South Twenty-second Street
Philadelphia, Pennsylvania 19103-4399

Visit Mary Hunt on the web!
www.cheapskatemonthly.com

Visit us on the web!
www.runningpress.com

CONTENTS

6   Introduction

10   Automobiles

20   Babies and Kids

32   Books and Computers

42   Cleaning

70   Clothing

80   Food and Cooking

108   Garage and Patio

114   Gifts

126   Grocery Shopping

138   Health and Beauty

154   Home

178   Kitchen Tricks

196   Laundry

208   Money and Finance

226   Organization and Storage

242   Pets

252   Repair and Maintenance

262   Special Occasions and Holidays

282   Travel and Entertainment

298   Yard and Garden

INTRODUCTION

People call me a cheapskate, and contrary to what you might assume, I like it! It reminds me that I'm not what I used to be: a credit-card junkie. Yes, I've come a long way from those days when I plunged my family so deeply into debt there was no seeming way we would ever get out. But we did. And I learned that living below one's means is an art, a way of life, a discipline that can be learned. In the same way I five- and ten-dollared myself to the brink of financial disaster, I worked my way back to financial solvency by watching all the expenses—especially the little ones. I didn't file for bankruptcy; I paid back every nickel of more than $100,000 of consumer debt (plus all the interest, fees, and penalties), and now I live to help others do the same.

Every day thousands of people from around the world read my newspaper column, *Everyday Cheapskate*, syndicated by Newspaper Enterprise Association. Four days a week it's my turn to encourage and motivate my readers to manage their money well. And on the fifth day I open the Mail Bag so my clever readers can share their tips for saving time and money. *Everyday Cheapskate* readers love tips! So do I. I often wonder who benefits more from my column: my readers or me. For sure, writing regularly about how to get out of debt, how to manage an ordinary income in an extraordinary world, and the joy and rewards of living below one's means keeps me on track. It would be easy to fall back into my old spendthrift ways.

And so for your enjoyment and reading pleasure, here is a little book packed full of unusual and particularly clever ways that my readers have taught all of us to save time and money . . . every day!

Mary Hunt
California

AUTOMOBILES

A car can be a money pit as well as a time waster, guzzling cash out of your bank account and demanding extra hours of your time for maintenance. But by taking a few preventive measures and making smart moves with your money and minutes, you can make this four-wheeled resource work best for you every day. Here are some clever car tips that will help you considerably over the long haul. Some of them even start to work before you leave the driveway!

Everyday Cheapskate's Greatest Tips

CONTENTS—AUTOMOBILES

13	Slash Insurance Costs
13	Gas Gouge
14	Cruise Control Caution
14	Bug and Tar Remover
14	Call First
15	Car Clean-Up
15	Car Help
16	Frugal Fragrance
16	Customized Car Mats
17	Gas Guidelines
17	Best Route
18	Soda Pop Clean Up
18	Whitewall Wonder
18	Frost-Free Windshield
19	Zap Sap
19	Keyed Up

SLASH INSURANCE COSTS

It pays to search online for auto insurance coverage. Visit sites like www.insweb.com, www.insurance.com, and www.esurance.com. Based on your answers to a few questions, you will be presented with a list of companies willing to provide online quotes immediately. Select the cheapest, and then call your company. Tell the agent what you have found (you will need details of the coverage), and then ask him to meet or beat it. If the company doesn't want to lose you, they'll beat it.

GAS GOUGE

Never fill up at the gas station closest to an Interstate exit. It is not unusual for gas stations on either side of the Interstate to charge at least 20 cents per gallon more than the stations right down the road. This can translate to a difference of $5 or more when filling up the tank of your car.

CRUISE CONTROL CAUTION

If you are in the habit of using the cruise control on your car (which saves on gas on the open road), don't use it on wet roads. If the tires hydroplane, the cruise keeps increasing the speed of the car. So when the tire bites and gets traction again the car will skid and swerve. No fun unless you're a stunt driver!

BUG AND TAR REMOVER

Use baking soda on a damp rag to remove bugs, tar, and anything else from a car's paint, grill, and chrome trim. Works better than pricey commercial products, leaves no residue or odor, and won't harm the paint. Just rinse off.

CALL FIRST

Call your insurance agent first before purchasing a new or used car. The price differential between makes and models of cars can be astounding. The last thing you want is to buy a nice two-door sedan and then find out the insurance industry considers it a sports car.

CAR CLEAN-UP

Place an old bath towel, bath mat, pillowcase, or table cloth under your baby's car seat. Now when your precious little one tosses food or a bottle onto the seat, the spread will protect the upholstery. Just throw it into the laundry for a quick and easy cleanup.

CAR HELP

Before shopping for a car—either new or used—log on to www.edmunds.com. This site offers a wealth of useful information to take with you when you go car shopping. Edmunds has a thorough checklist you can print out to remind you to reconsider each little detail about a used car.

FRUGAL FRAGRANCE

If you love scented candles, now you can enjoy them in your car without striking a match. There's always a glob of wax left over when the wick has burned through. Put the wax glob on a paper plate and cut it into chunks with a butter knife. Find an old clean sock, put the scented chunks into the sock and tie a knot in the end. Put the sock under your car seat.

CUSTOMIZED CAR MATS

Floor mats for a mini-van can be outrageously expensive through your car dealership. Discount department stores offer reasonable prices on mats, but they do not fit well. Try using the clear plastic runner material that is available by the yard at home improvement centers. With a utility knife you can cut this to fit around the seat hardware to create a tight fit. This can save a lot of money and works beautifully.

GAS GUIDELINES

Most gas stations offer Unleaded Premium for 10 to 12 cents a gallon more than Unleaded Regular. Many customers think they're giving their car some kind of extra care or a "treat" by filling up with what they think is the best. Don't do it. Virtually all automobiles run just fine on Unleaded Regular; so unless your vehicle's documentation specifically states that it requires a premium grade of gas with higher octane, save your money and stick with regular.

BEST ROUTE

If you have several alternate routes you can take to work or school each day, you might be surprised to find that the shortest route might not be the fastest. And by doing a little math, you'll find that getting up a little earlier can save you big bucks on gas and avoid wear and tear on your car, not to mention miles on your odometer.

SODA POP CLEAN UP

If you need to remove spilled soda pop from your car interior, try cleaning with a 50/50 mixture of vinegar and water and a toothbrush. You will be surprised that this solution will take out upholstery stains that stumped even professional car detailers.

WHITEWALL WONDER

Try Lysol Basin Tub and Tile Cleaner on your cars' whitewalls. It works great and is much cheaper than buying a product specifically for car tires. It makes the tires look great with only a small amount of elbow grease.

FROST-FREE WINDSHIELD

Nothing's worse than having to chip away the ice on your car windows when it is freezing outside. So eliminate the frost on your windshield (not to mention your eyelids) with a little preventative care. Wipe your windshields and windows with straight white vinegar after you park for the evening to help keep ice and frost at bay. Not only will your car thank you, but your skin will, too.

ZAP SAP

A cheap and safe way to remove pine tree sap from your car without damaging the finish is to rub it with a soft cloth soaked with plain 70 percent isopropyl (rubbing) alcohol, available at the pharmacy or drug store for less than a dollar.

KEYED UP

The keyless remote for my car died so I stopped by the Honda dealership to pick up a new battery. I left empty-handed when I saw the price: $50 for a replacement battery! I opened the remote myself by removing the tiny screw, pulled out the battery, stopped by a department store and picked up a replacement for $1.77. It's good as new.

BABIES AND KIDS

Babies are truly a bundle of joy, but they also cost a bundle of money. Of course, they're worth every dime, and all the time you spend raising your children is time well spent. While every child has a seemingly endless list of needs—including food and clothes and toys and special furniture, to say the least—there's an equally long list of wise alternative ways to fill those needs while keeping your child safe, healthy, and happy. Read on for some of my favorite, most ingenious tips for childrearing the cheapskate way.

CONTENTS—BABIES AND KIDS

23	Rash Soother
23	Beach Bag
23	Rainbow Bath
24	Creative Changing Table
24	Diaper Rash
25	Repurposed Baby Blankets
25	Double Notes
26	Cheap Ball Pit
26	Homemade Wipes
27	Love Luvs
27	Picture Postcard
28	Pool Decals
28	Replacement Parts
29	Slick Bang Trim
29	Soak on the Go
30	Sturdy Backpacks
30	Toy Links
31	Kids Shoe Saver

RASH SOOTHER

Here's yet another tip using that all-purpose miracle product, baking soda. One-half cup baking soda in a warm bath is an excellent soother for diaper rash. Let the skin air dry after the bath, and the baby's bottom is on its way to well.

BEACH BAG

Take a large zipper-type plastic bag to the beach with ¼ cup of baking soda inside. Use it to bring home wet swimsuits. Just put them in the bag and shake. The soda absorbs moisture and helps prevent mildew and scary smells until you can get the suits properly laundered.

RAINBOW BATH

Young children love those commercials' colored bath crystals for kids that turn bath water into various colors. Rather than pay $10 for bath crystals, experiment. Just two drops of plain blue food coloring turns a bath a beautiful aquamarine color. Your little ones will be thrilled with the blue water, and emerge clean, without a trace of color on their skin.

CREATIVE CHANGING TABLE

Can't find a sturdy and inexpensive changing table? Try building one. Purchase an oak workbench kit at the local hardware store (very affordable). When you put it together, place a quarter-inch layer of foam padding from a fabric center on the top surface. Place a rubber-backed fabric over the foam, tuck it under the tabletop, and staple it in place to the underside. You will have a high-quality piece of furniture with more work surface than the typical changing station, and also two shelves for diapers, wipes, and a baby tub. As a bonus, when your child no longer needs a changing table you'll have a great workbench.

DIAPER RASH

Instead of expensive commercial ointments to treat diaper

rash, try this: Mix a quarter-cup petroleum jelly with one tablespoon cornstarch (more or less to suit your preference). This makes a creamy paste similar to expensive commercial products and works great on a baby's tender areas.

REPURPOSED BABY BLANKETS

When your children outgrow those tiny receiving blankets, don't get rid of the blankets. Repurpose them by sewing them together into larger blankets for their beds. This will not only save you money, but will provide your children with comfort for many years to come.

DOUBLE NOTES

Keep a message pad that makes duplicate copies for sending notes to your child's teacher, bus driver, or troop leader. You can find these at any office supply store. The duplicate copy makes a handy reference should you need to follow-up later.

CHEAP BALL PIT

Kids of every age love to play in those silly ball "pits." You can make one for your kids. Purchase a small, round inflatable wading pool for less than $4 at your local discount store. Add 150 balls for around $20. Now you have a portable ball pit that works inside or out for less than $25.

HOMEMADE WIPES

You can make your own high-quality baby wipes quite easily. With a serrated knife, carefully cut a roll of good quality paper towels (like Bounty) in half horizontally so you have two short rolls, about the size of toilet tissue. Put one of the short rolls into a No. 9 Rubbermaid container. Gently mix together 2 cups hot water, 2 tablespoons mineral oil, and 1 tablespoon Johnson's baby shampoo. Pour this mixture over the towels and allow all of it to be absorbed by the towels. Pull out cardboard core from the center. To use, pull a towel from the center of the roll and tear off.

Reseal between uses. These wipes are great for make-up removal, too.

LOVE LUVS

Disposable diapers can be so costly. You can save a lot of money by purchasing Luvs because they are cut wider and you can buy the smaller size longer. The smaller sizes come with more diapers per pack for the same price as the next larger size.

PICTURE POSTCARD

When your child has a birthday party, snap a photo of the birthday child with the gift and the child who gave it. Instead of writing out thank you cards, have the child write his or her thanks on the right half on the back of the picture. Address on the left, affix postage at the postcard rate and mail without an envelope.

POOL DECALS

Stores everywhere provide ways to cut down on bathtub slips. There is no reason why you shouldn't apply those some products to other wet surfaces, such as kiddy pools. Put bathtub decals on the bottom of a kiddy pool to make it less slippery. The decal should work double duty, not you.

REPLACEMENT PARTS

Ever found a brand new game at a tag sale for only a few bucks but it was missing a few parts? Take a chance and snap it up. You'll be glad you did. Hasbro, www.hasbro.com, offers replacement parts for all kinds of board games, including Monopoly. Click on "Customer Service" and then "Replacement Parts." You can get extra dice and Monopoly tokens for $2. Or how about a Boggle timer? Also $2. Two bucks will get you a bag of spare parts for The Game of Life (six cars, people pegs, and a spinner arm). Hasbro sells parts for all kinds of games, including many from Milton Bradley and Parker Brothers, too.

SLICK BANG TRIM

Tired of paying salon prices for your daughter's bang trim? Try this: Place a piece of Scotch tape across the bangs and cut along the bottom edge. The tape keeps the hair nice and straight and you can step back and see if the tape placement is correct and straight before starting to cut. Your little one will be so curious about what you're doing it's quite possible that she'll sit still until you are done.

SOAK ON THE GO

If your infant or toddler occasionally soils a garment while you are away from home, try this trick to keep the stain from setting. Put two tablespoons of powdered Dreft (or your detergent of choice) and one tablespoon of Biz in a gallon size zip-type bag and keep it in your diaper bag.

Put the soiled garment in the bag, add water, zip the seal tightly closed, and shake to mix everything together. When you get home, the garment has been presoaked and is ready to wash.

STURDY BACKPACKS

Many kids have terrible problems with backpacks. Most fall apart. Even the expensive ones can't make it through an entire school season. Your solution may be in an Army/Navy surplus store. You will find military backpacks that wear like iron. In fact, your kids could carry them for years, all the way through high school. And they look very cool.

TOY LINKS

You no longer need to fret about losing your child's favorite toy, or your money. Shower curtain rings work perfectly for attaching baby toys to strollers, car seats, etc.

At $1.29 for a package of 12, it's a great savings over links sold specifically for this purpose that run about 50 cents each.

KIDS SHOE SAVER

Kids can be very hard on tennis shoes. Whenever their leather or canvas shoes start looking a little ragged, use 1 tablespoon of Soft Scrub cleaner on a clean smooth rag and wipe the scuff marks, chewing gum, play dough, and dirt from the smooth part of the shoes. Don't use on colored shoes because there is a small amount of bleach in Soft Scrub.

BOOKS
AND COMPUTERS

Books will always be a necessity, but now that the computer age is here (practically every home has one) we all face costs that our parents never really did. From all the hardware it takes to get started, to all the software it takes to get anything done, to everything in between, computers are an expensive addition to the family budget. And because the majority of people have only been "online" for about a decade now, many don't know enough to maximize their computer's ability while minimizing cost. Try these intelligent tips for saving time and money in the information age.

CONTENTS—BOOKS AND COMPUTERS

35	Free Bestsellers
35	Book Smarts
36	Empty Ink Cartridges
36	Freecycle It
37	Get Froogled
38	Inkjet Life Extension
38	Run EZ Wizard
39	Get Organized
39	Stretch that Ink
40	Support the Library
40	411 on Directory Assistance
41	Visit the Library

FREE BESTSELLERS

The next time you go book shopping, take a paper and pen along, and head for the current best-selling paperback section. Write down the titles and authors of the top 10 titles that interest you. But don't purchase any of them. Take your list to the library and borrow those books. Most of the time you will find the titles you want, as well as previous titles by the same author that you may have missed. If the latest title by a popular author is not yet in stock, put your name on the waiting list. By the time you've read the books you check out, that new release will be ready.

BOOK SMARTS

Love to read but don't have the time to go to the library? Don't drain your budget or clutter your shelves. Enroll in www.booksfree.com. They have an entire inventory of mass market paperbacks you can borrow free by paying a monthly fee for shipping and handling of $6.99, which is less than the cost of one new book. They'll ship you two books at a time. When you're done reading both (no due dates, no late fees), return them in the prepaid mailer they came in. Automatically you will receive the next two books on your reading list.

EMPTY INK CARTRIDGES

If your printer announces "Low Ink!" during the middle of a job, you can finish and even buy yourself a couple more days of printing: Remove the cartridge from the printer, give it a good shake and replace it in the printer. You'll be amazed how many more pages you can print on an "empty" ink cartridge.

FREECYCLE IT

There is a website where you can recycle your clutter. Freecycling is giving away your clutter to someone else who wants it. Freecycle Yahoo Groups have sprung up all around the world. If there isn't one in your local area, you can start a group. It's easy. If you've got something to give away, you post it on your local Freecycle board. If a member wants it, he or she contacts you and the two of you make arrangements for pickup. Find out more about freecycling at www.freecycle.org.

GET FROOGLED

Froogle is an excellent free service from Google, the Internet search engine. With Froogle you can comparison shop all kinds of online stores, including the biggies like Amazon and Barnes and Noble. You can set price ranges in your search, look in certain categories, and find just about everything. Go to Google.com and click on Froogle. Now type in the item you want. You can be specific with brand, model and color. Froogle will produce a list of many places where the item can be purchased, ranked by price. Now you know how to decide which merchant is the most affordable.

INKJET LIFE EXTENSION

A computer technician will tell you that you should never replace your ink or toner cartridge just because the light is flashing. Wait until you can actually see the effects on the page you are printing. Many laser printers will work well for two or three weeks after it says "Toner Low" and with no degradation in the print quality. And if you wait too long, and you do get a bad print job, so what? One page of ruined text costs about two cents versus hundreds of dollars in cartridges thrown away prematurely.

RUN EZ WIZARD

If you computer doesn't have "sleep mode" where it automatically goes into an energy-saving sleep after a certain time of inactivity, you can get EZ Wizard free of charge from www.energystar.gov/powermanagement/wizard.asp?orgtype . Just download it and start racking up the savings: you'll cut down on wear and tear on your computer and put a slight but worthwhile dent in your energy bill.

GET ORGANIZED

With the relatively low cost of computers, scanners, and CD burners, you can take personal record maintenance to a new level. Scan your personal documents into the computer as jpeg files. Then burn two copies onto CDs. Keep one at home and the other as a back-up in a safe or deposit box. You can also do this for tax return documentation. You will save on space and also gain peace of mind from the knowledge that all of your important papers are safe and "filed" neatly.

STRETCH THAT INK

When printing to-do lists, weekly chore lists for your children, the grocery list, weekly menus, and other items you need for a short time, you can extend the life of your printer's ink supply by setting the font color to gray instead of black. You will still be able to read what you've printed, but you'll be using much less ink. That means fewer cartridge changes.

SUPPORT THE LIBRARY

If your Internet provider's charges are killing your budget, you might do what we did: cancel it and send your kids to use the library computers. If they wonder what's going on, tell them you are saving for their college tuition.

411 ON DIRECTORY ASSISTANCE

Telephone books are difficult to manage because they're so big and bulky, and are quickly out-of-date. But calling directory assistance can get expensive—$1.50 per call or more. Ouch! Here's a better idea. Look up numbers and addresses (even driving directions) for people and businesses at websites like www.anywho.com,

www.superpages.com, www.switchboard.com, and
www.infousa.com. They're free.

VISIT THE LIBRARY

What a fabulous place the library is. There you and your
kids will find current newspapers, magazines, children's
books, adult books, videos, VCR's, cassettes, CD's, and
wonderful story-tellers. If you like to shop for fun, satisfy
the impulse by visiting a library. You can take home something new, and it doesn't cost anything. Bonus tip: Some
libraries have added cake pans in the shape of characters.
You can check them out to make your kids' birthday cakes
in the same way you borrow books. Just remember to be
considerate and return it in like condition to that which you
borrowed it. Other people will be grateful and so will you
if you ever need it again.

CLEANING

Cleaning is the one chore that most of us abhor, but we all know it has to be done. And while none of the cheapskate cleaning methods my readers have offered pretend to make it fun, they do promise to cut costs and save time. Also, most of these tips can be implemented with everyday items you probably already have. From creative uses of everything from lemon juice to rubbing alcohol to baking soda to simple table salt and more, my favorite time- and money-saving cleaning tips are presented here for your purifying pleasure.

CONTENTS—CLEANING

47	Add Lemon
47	Sink Cleanser
47	Silver Cleaner
48	Casserole Cleanup
48	Disinfecting Solution
49	Marble Cleaner
49	Make-Up Stains
50	Odor Eater
50	Whiteboard Cleaner
50	Glass Coffee Pot Cleaner
51	Gunk Be Gone
51	Bathroom Drain Dissolver
52	Scum Solution
52	Bye-Bye Mildew
52	Wax Remover
53	Cheap Glass Cleaner
53	Dishwasher Cleaner
54	Power Clean
54	Clean Oven Racks
54	Clean Your Iron
55	Club Soda Clean-Up

55	Copper Cleaner
56	Crayon Mark Magic
56	Plant Shine
56	Decal Remover
57	Denture Clean
57	Disposable Apron
58	D.I.Y. Sanitizing Wipes
58	Double Duty
59	Drawer Freshener
59	Floor Cleaner
59	Glass Cleaner
60	Hairspray Spots
60	Iron Cleaner
61	Iron Residue Remover
61	Hairbrush Clean-Up
62	Stubborn Toilet Stains
62	Marble Stain Remover
63	Remove Price Labels
63	Paintbrush Cleaner
63	Porcelain Stain Remover
64	Toilet Cleaner

64   Musty Smells

65   Rust Out

65   Scum Gone

66   Soap Scum Remover

66   Shampoo the Doors

66   Soft Scrub Sub

67   Spray Cleaner

67   Swiffer Sub

68   Window Washing

68   Wood Cleaner

68   Clorox Ready Mop Replacement

ADD LEMON

Salt and ice together are great for cleaning the stains from the inside of pots, carafes, and thermoses. For really tough jobs, add either lemon juice or a couple of lemon wedges to the ice cubes and salt. Whirl all of that together. The acid in lemon juice helps to break down all the gunk.

SINK CLEANSER

If you run out of cleanser, don't panic. It's only an opportunity to think outside of the box and try other materials. Try baking soda—it works like a charm. It will even take care of the ring in the bathtub with amazing results.

SILVER CLEANER

To clean your silver without harsh commercial chemical products, use the miracle powder in your pantry: baking soda. Make a thick paste of baking soda and water, and massage it gently into your silver products with an old, soft toothbrush. Rinse in warm soapy water and dry well. Warning: You may never go back to $10 cleaners once you try the 50-cent solution.

CASSEROLE CLEANUP

To make quick work of cleaning a nasty baked on casserole dish, fill it with hot water and add a fabric softener sheet to the water. Let it soak for a while. The gunk will just slide out. You can even get extra mileage from a sheet that has already gone through the dryer cycle.

DISINFECTING SOLUTION

It's important to disinfect cutting boards and counter tops, especially when working with poultry and meat products. Instead of buying expensive kitchen disinfectants, make your own: Combine ½ teaspoon liquid chlorine bleach to one quart of water. Dispense from a clean spray bottle. Flood the food cutting surface with the solution, let stand several minutes, then wash and rinse. More bleach is not better. This is the perfect ratio of bleach to water to kill bacteria and not leave bleach spots on kitchen linens.

MARBLE CLEANER

Marble is a very delicate product that can be easily damaged. Never use acidic products like vinegar or lemon juice on marble. It will etch the surface and destroy the finish. Instead, clean marble with a sponge, soft cloth, or mop and a neutral cleaner like Murphy's Oil Soap or even liquid dishwashing detergent mixed with warm water.

MAKE-UP STAINS

There's nothing so stubborn as make-up stains on white face cloths. You can remove them easily and cheaply with Fels Naptha bar soap, which is available in the laundry aisle of most grocery stores. It works like magic. Simply wet a corner of the bar and rub it on the stain. Launder as usual. A bar of Fels Naptha will last for years in your laundry room.

ODOR EATER

Here's how to get the odor out of just about anything, including stinky coolers, glass jars and musty drawers. Dampen a paper towel and set it into a small container. Pour two teaspoons of cheap vanilla extract on it. Put the whole thing inside the smelly container and close it. Wait for three days. This really works great, even inside old refrigerators.

WHITEBOARD CLEANER

Use WD-40 to clean dry-erase markings from a white-board. It works very well and leaves no dry-erase "ghosts."

GLASS COFFEE POT CLEANER

If you've ever worked in a restaurant that serves a lot of coffee, you're bound to know this handy trick to keep the pots looking fresh and new. Pour about 2 tablespoons of salt into the empty carafe plus enough ice to fill the pot about ⅓ full. Vigorously swirl the contents in a circular motion and the stains and burned-on coffee lift right off. When finished, dump the contents, and finish with dish-washing liquid and water.

GUNK BE GONE

Pots with burned-on food won't be a problem if you do this: Fill with warm water and throw in a couple of dryer sheets. Let stand for 20 minutes to several hours. The mess will all slide out like magic. Just make sure you don't let that sheet go down the drain or the garbage disposal.

BATHROOM DRAIN DISSOLVER

To help dissolve scum and hair in your sluggish bathroom sink and tub drains, pour a mixture of 1 cup salt, 1 cup baking soda, and ½ cup white vinegar into the drain. Allow to stand for 15 minutes, then flush with 2 quarts of boiling water followed by flushing hot tap water down the drain for 1 minute. You can repeat this process if necessary.

SCUM SOLUTION

Sometimes the simple solutions work the best. Plain powdered borax (sold as Twenty Mule Team in many supermarkets) works well to remove scum from tubs and showers. Use as you would any powdered cleanser.

BYE-BYE MILDEW

Tired of buying new shower curtains only to surrender them to the same fate—mildew build-up? To prevent mildew from forming on a new shower curtain, soak it in salt water before hanging for the first time. Keep the curtain and say goodbye to the mildew.

WAX REMOVER

To remove candle wax from carpets, try this: Using a cool iron, place paper towels over the affected area and carefully iron the paper. Repeat until the paper no longer becomes opaque. Use fresh paper if necessary.

CHEAP GLASS CLEANER

Windshield washer fluid is often available for as little as 89 cents a gallon. It is a much weaker solution than Windex and does not contain ammonia. Still, it will do a good job on lightly soiled mirrors and windows, crystal chandeliers, and jewelry at quite a bargain.

DISHWASHER CLEANER

Keep your dishwasher looking like new on the inside by simply pouring a small package (25 cents) of unsweetened Lemonade Kool-Aid powder into the soap dispenser and run it empty for a complete cycle. The citric acid in the Kool-Aid removes all the hard water stains and leaves it sparkling white. This is much cheaper than Tang ($4 or more), which does about the same thing. Do this twice a year.

POWER CLEAN

Mix rubbing alcohol and water 50/50 in a spray bottle to make a powerful all-purpose cleaner. It leaves no streaks, and it kills germs. Store brand rubbing alcohol is particularly affordable. Caution: May damage painted surfaces.

CLEAN OVEN RACKS

Another way to clean oven racks is to put them into a large garbage bag, throw in a cup of ammonia, and tightly seal the bag. Let the racks sit overnight. The burned on gunk cleans up easily in the morning. Just make sure you place the bag in a ventilated area and on a floor that cannot be damaged, such as outback or in the garage with open windows.

CLEAN YOUR IRON

Table salt can easily remove the gunk that builds up on the surface of your household iron. Sprinkle a little salt on a piece of wax paper or a soft cloth and run the hot iron over it to remove all the buildup. Repeat as necessary. Works like sandpaper without scratching.

CLUB SODA CLEAN-UP

For a fast clean-up after a party, use up that leftover club soda to clean and shine glass, chrome, and appliances. Apply with paper towel or a soft cloth as you would any glass cleaner. In just a few moments, you can be prepared to serve the whole party all over again.

COPPER CLEANER

Copper can be tricky. So here's an easy tip you might want to share with your friends, and you'll definitely want to try yourself: Clean copper-bottom pots with a paste made of salt and vinegar. (Do not use this on decorative copper that has a lacquer coating.)

CRAYON MARK MAGIC

You can transform your walls back to normal after they have served as canvases for your child's great art expression. A good paste car wax will remove crayon marks from painted surfaces without damaging the surface at all. Simply rub on the car wax, allow it to soften and absorb crayon wax, buff off, and then follow with an all-purpose cleaner to remove any residue. It works great!

PLANT SHINE

Instead of using a waxy, expensive houseplant shine-mist, a dab of mayonnaise on a soft rag will clean and shine flat leafed houseplants in a jiffy. Gently polish the top surface of the leaf only. Do not use this on fuzzy type plants like African violets.

DECAL REMOVER

Remove shower/tub rubber "decals" with WD-40, available

in a spray can in the automotive department of stores like Wal-Mart and Target (even in some supermarkets). It is an excellent solvent for all adhesives. Once removed, clean the tub surface well to remove all traces of the WD-40.

DENTURE CLEAN

Carefully fill a Thermos, vase, or other vessel that has a build-up of stain or hard water minerals with boiling water and drop in a denture-cleaning tablet (or add a teaspoonful of denture cleaning powder). Stir and leave for a couple of hours (even overnight); then rinse thoroughly. Works like a charm.

DISPOSABLE APRON

If you have a particularly dirty job to do—like cleaning the outdoor grill, taking down dirty window screens, or hosing down the patio furniture—make yourself a disposable apron to spare your good ones. Take a large garbage bag, cut holes for your head and arms, and slip it over your clothes. You may look a little weird, but you'll protect your clothes and save yourself a lot of time and trouble later.

D.I.Y. SANITIZING WIPES

Disinfecting wipes are great for quick bathroom cleanups, but they're expensive—about 13 cents per wipe on average. So make your own. Tear off a whole roll of paper towels and stack them in a plastic container that has a tight-fitting lid. Pour about 3 cups of Lysol multi-purpose liquid cleaner over the roll and apply the lid. Now you have convenient bathroom wipes for less than 2 cents each.

DOUBLE DUTY

Instead of buying a mop bucket (which also takes up a lot of room) use your small trash cans as mop buckets. Rotate each week so that each of your trash cans get a regular, thorough cleaning, just like your floors.

DRAWER FRESHENER

To sweeten old musty drawers, scrub the inside surfaces with a 50/50 mixture of chlorine bleach and water. Allow to dry and air in a well-ventilated area. Use rubber gloves and eye protection when applying, and be careful to not allow the mix to splash onto carpet or fabrics that will be permanently damaged.

FLOOR CLEANER

Wash your vinyl and ceramic tile floors with a mixture of 1 cup white vinegar to 1 gallon of hot water. There is no need to rinse, and you will never have that nasty film that plain water leaves behind.

GLASS CLEANER

You can make a good glass and window cleaner yourself with this recipe: 45 percent water, 45 percent rubbing alcohol and 10 percent household ammonia. Exact measurements are not important. Put it in a clearly marked spray bottle. This is as good as any product you can buy.

HAIRSPRAY SPOTS

Who says shaving cream is just for our bodies? You can use shaving cream to remove hairspray from walls, woodwork, and mirrors in your bathroom. It works great and leaves no nasty fumes or smells.

IRON CLEANER

Clean your steam iron from the inside out. Fill the steam reservoir with white vinegar and heat to the hottest setting. The iron is going to steam vinegar, so get prepared for a strong smell. You will see all kinds of hard water deposits come out of the steam holes. Once empty, fill with water and allow to steam well to remove all traces of vinegar. Repeat as necessary.

IRON RESIDUE REMOVER

Here's a great way to remove residue from the soleplate of your iron. Mix baking soda and water into a paste. Dip a damp cloth into the mixture and rub it gently on the soleplate. Clean it off with a dry cloth. If you still have residue, clean the iron with a paste of mild cleanser and water, and then wipe with a damp cloth. Flush out any remaining cleanser by turning on the iron and pressing the steam control button.

HAIRBRUSH CLEAN-UP

Fill a large glass or other container with warm water. Add 2 tablespoons liquid fabric softener or two dryer sheets. Stir. Then, add combs and hair brushes. Allow them to soak for a few hours. Hair spray and other hair products will be released from implements so you can simply rinse them with little or no scrubbing.

STUBBORN TOILET STAINS

Try a Mr. Clean Magic Eraser on those ugly stains in the toilet that even pumice stones won't get out. Put on your gloves and go to work, but only after you have read the instructions carefully.

MARBLE STAIN REMOVER

To remove a food or beverage stain left on a marble table-top, make a paste of hydrogen peroxide (hair-bleaching strength available at a beauty supply store) and whiting (an abrasive powder available at hardware stores). Add a few drops of clear household ammonia. Spread the paste on the stained area of the marble, cover with plastic wrap and let it stand for several hours. Rinse. Repeat as necessary until the stain is gone.

Cleaning

REMOVE PRICE LABELS

To remove a sticky price label, apply a small amount of
cooking oil to remove it. Just apply with your fingertip and
rub the spot a little, then wipe with a clean paper towel and
the residue will come right off. Rubbing alcohol works
similarly on particular glass and porcelain surfaces.

PAINTBRUSH CLEANER

To remove paint from a paintbrush, make a mixture of ½
cup liquid fabric softener per gallon of warm water. Swish
the brush vigorously in the liquid while counting to 10.
Remove the brush and there will be no paint on the brush.
Rinse in clear water, shake out the water and allow to dry.

PORCELAIN STAIN REMOVER

To remove hard water marks and stains from porcelain
sinks and tubs without scratching the surfaces, mix 1 cup

salt with 1 cup baking soda and keep it in a sealed container. Use the mixture as you would any scouring powder.

TOILET CLEANER

To save all that money you spend on toilet bowl cleaners and still eliminate the stains from inside your toilet bowl, use a cheap pumice stone. Pumice stones are available in the drugstore or hardware store. Simply don a pair of rubber or latex surgical gloves and use the pumice stone the way you would a sponge or other scrubbing device.

MUSTY SMELLS

Here's one antique dealer's secret for removing musty smells from old pieces of furniture. Place a slice of white bread on a saucer and cover it with white distilled vinegar. Place the saucer inside the drawer or cabinet and close. The smell will absorb into the mixture.

RUST OUT

If you have stubborn red rust stains or other metal oxide stains in a garment or other fabric item, oxalic acid is the way to go. There are two products in the stores that contain oxalic acid: Bar Keepers Friend and Zud. Mix a paste of the product and rub it into the stain. Keep the paste damp for 30 minutes or more, and it will remove the rust. Then rinse it out with plain water. It's always a good idea to test the product on a hidden portion of the fabric. But a white shirt with a rust stain is worthless anyway.

SCUM GONE

The easiest way to remove soap scum in a tub or shower is with Calgon water softener, which can be found in the detergent section of most supermarkets. Apply a small amount to a wet cloth. Rub on, rinse off, scum is gone. This works so well and is so mild that you can do this while taking a shower without hurting your skin at all.

SOAP SCUM REMOVER

Mineral or lemon oil removes soap scum quickly and easily and keeps it from coming back. Just wipe onto doors and walls to remove the spots, and then polish the surface with a soft cloth. The next time you take a shower you'll be amazed to see how the water runs right off. Repeat as necessary. Caution: Cover the floor of the tub or shower before applying oil to prevent a dangerous slipping hazard.

SHAMPOO THE DOORS

Apply cheap shampoo to a wet wash cloth and rub on shower doors and walls to remove soap scum buildup. This will make your shower doors crystal clean and beautiful. And you can do this while taking a shower.

SOFT SCRUB SUB

Why spend $4 to $5 a bottle for liquid cleansers like Soft Scrub when you can make your own? Just find an empty

bottle, add a 50-cent can of Ajax, Comet, or Bon Ami powdered cleanser, add warm water, and shake. Works great
and no more wet and clogged cleanser cans in the shower.

SPRAY CLEANER

To make a very effective spray cleaner put a half-capful of
liquid Spic-n-Span in an empty spray bottle and top it off
with water. The mixture will clean as well as a highly concentrated version and does not require a final rinse. At this
rate, one bottle of Spic-n-Span liquid will last for a very
long time.

SWIFFER SUB

Huggies baby wipes (about 3 cents each) are close to the
same size and texture as the replacement cloth for the
Swiffer dry mop (which cost about 25 cents each). Wash a
new Huggies wipe to remove the oils first. They're very
durable and work as well as the Swiffer replacement
cloths.

WINDOW WASHING

An excellent cheap way to clean windows and mirrors to a sparkling shine is to spray on a 50/50 mixture of white vinegar and water. Buff dry with crumpled newspaper. No streaks or smears.

WOOD CLEANER

Baby wipes are an excellent dirt remover for wood. Slightly oily, they clean up much more dirt than wood soaps or wood polishes. Works great on wood paneling.

CLOROX READY MOP REPLACEMENT

A strong paper towel, like Brawny, works great in place of the Clorox Ready Mop replacement sheet. Tear away a bit of the towel to allow for the spray holes.

CLOTHING

Keeping the family in quality threads is no mean feat these days. But if you're willing to be a smart shopper and a willing mender, you'll see that there are countless ways to stretch your clothing dollar while keeping a closet ful of the latest fashions for every season. From hanger know-how and static-cling control to smart shopping strategies and savvy alteration ideas, *Everyday Cheapskate* readers from across the continent have provided some great ways to look fine with an eye on the bottom line.

CONTENTS—CLOTHING

73	Belt Adjustment
73	Darning Thread
73	Pattern Paper
74	Hanger Hooray
74	Hanger How-To
75	Moth Repellent
75	Re-Heel
75	Prevent Runs
76	New Zip
76	Good-Bye Static
77	Clean Whites
77	Ugly No More
78	Debit Merchandise

BELT ADJUSTMENT

Discount clothing stores like Ross, T.J. Maxx, and
Marshalls are great places to find designer name-brand
men's leather belts that retail in department stores for $50-
$80, for $20 or less. The problem is they usually have only
large sizes. Don't worry. Pick out the one you like then
take it to a shoe repair shop for shortening. It should cost
less than $5 to have the buckle removed, belt shortened,
and buckle reattached.

DARNING THREAD

Darning thread is difficult to find these days. But if you
still mend your socks or other clothes in this manner, use
embroidery floss. Divide the six strands into one or two, to
suit you. It comes in all colors and is very cheap.

PATTERN PAPER

Use the plastic liners from cereal boxes for craft and

sewing patterns. A pattern made from this material can be pinned on many times without tearing and can be neatly folded for storage.

HANGER HOORAY

Most department stores are eager to give away their excess hangers. Ask for the hangers with your purchases, and request any extras behind the counter. The men's department will have larger hangers, and the children's department small ones.

HANGER HOW-TO

When hanging suit jackets or blazers on a commercial wooden hanger that has a curved shape, place the hanger backwards with the curved side toward you. Then hang the suit jacket or blazer facing you. Placing the hanger backwards keeps the shape of the shoulders in a sturdier, tighter position and that means fewer professional pressings will be required.

MOTH REPELLENT

Buy a bag of cedar chips (the kind used in animal pet cages for bedding). Stuff the cedar chips into old knee-hi's. Tie at the top with ribbon or string, leaving a loop to hang on a hanger in your closet. You can also place these in a drawer or box where you store winter clothes. Cedar is a natural pest repellant, and the chips are much cheaper than cedar sold for this purpose.

RE-HEEL

Instead of buying new dress shoes once the heels start to wear out, take them to a shoe repair shop and have the heels replaced for $5-$10. This greatly extends the life of a good pair of shoes and extends your paycheck, too.

PREVENT RUNS

Mix 2 cups of salt with 1 gallon of warm water. Immerse clean dry pantyhose. Soak for three hours or overnight.

Rinse the hose in cool water and allow to drip dry. (You can save the soaking liquid for future use.) The salt toughens the fibers, which makes them more resistant to snags and runs.

NEW ZIP

Zippers can wear out and slow down. This doesn't mean you have to replace the zipper or put up with it being difficult. To make a zipper slide up and down more smoothly, simply rub a candle over the teeth.

GOOD-BYE STATIC

During the winter, when static cling is a problem, keep a dryer sheet handy. Run a sheet over your hair to reverse the static. Do the same across the skirt or trousers you are wearing. Run that sheet across your legs if your petticoat is sticking. The problem will be solved. One sheet lasts for many uses; it also smells good, so stash it in your handbag.

CLEAN WHITES

After polishing and buffing white tennis shoes, I use an old Army trick and spray them lightly with clear shellac. They keep a nice polished look for a while and wipe clean easily.

UGLY NO MORE

I bought some shoes that I love at a clearance sale but the only problem was the ugly color. I'm hard to fit, so I bought them anyway. I bought a can of shoe color spray ($4 for a 4 oz. can) at the shoe repair shop. I sprayed the shoes black and they turned out beautifully. (It would have run $15 to have the shoe repair man spray them—more than the shoes cost!) The secret is to spray lightly and cover up the soles with masking tape. Recently, I sprayed a handbag ($220 marked down to $20) because of the ugly color, which is now gorgeous.

DEBIT MERCHANDISE

Make friends with the managers of your favorite stores, and you might be able to tap into a gold mine. Ask if their "debit" or used merchandise is available for sale. These are the items which have been returned for one reason or another (button fell off, customer wore it once and reattached the tags thinking they fooled the store, or for some other reason the customer wasn't happy and the retailer felt obligated to take it back and make a refund). These items cannot be put back on the floor or returned to the manufacturer. Typically these items are sold for pennies on the dollar.

FOOD AND COOKING

A friend of mine's grandmother always used to say, "If we didn't need food, we'd all be rich!" This may be true. But then, a life without food would be a little less pleasurable. Still, there are ample ways to make great food cheap, make perishable food last, and make the grocery budget stretch like nobody's business. Plus, the tips in this chapter are filled with practiced wisdom for practical solutions, novel ideas, and inspiring concepts that make cooking fun and rewarding for you and your family. *Bon appétit!*

Everyday Cheapskate's Greatest Tips

CONTENTS—FOOD AND COOKING

85	Bacon Rinse
85	Baking Powder Sub
85	Banana Preservation
86	Blended "Cheapuccino"
86	Brownie Secret
87	Brown Sugar Surrogate
87	Cake Mix Cookies
88	Cheese Saver
89	Cinnamon Coffee
89	Chocolate Chip Stand-In
89	Coffee Stretcher
90	Coke Marinade
90	Cracker Crumb Creation
91	Fake Egg
91	Quick Fat Removal
91	Ginger Fresh
92	Freezer Soup
92	Freshness Extended
93	Frozen Peppers
93	Frozen Whipped Cream
93	Grated Butter

94	Gourmet Coffee
94	Grow Some Yogurt
95	Ham-Bone Benefits
95	Handy Broth Cubes
96	Substitute Buttermilk
96	Quick Chocolate Mousse
96	Leftover Magician
97	Makin' Bacon
97	Meat Tenderizer
98	Milk Cubes
98	Sweet Milk
99	Egg Reduction
99	Noodle Know-How
100	Oven-Fried Bacon
100	Perfect Meatballs
101	Yogurt Substitute
101	Handy Milk
101	Pumpkin Puree
102	Pumpkin Seeds
103	Recycled Spuds
103	Secret Ingredient

Everyday Cheapskate's Greatest Tips

103   Self-Grating Cheese
104   Shortcut Spuds
104   Spinach Spice-Up
105   Stand-Up Chicken
105   Sugared Fruit
106   Super Fast, Super Fine
106   Thicken Gravy
106   Toned-Down Tomato Sauce
107   Wine Cook-Alikes

BACON RINSE

A strip of bacon never seems to go far, especially once it hits the frying pan. So rinse bacon under cold water before frying. This reduces the amount the bacon shrinks when cooked by almost 50 percent.

BAKING POWDER SUB

Before running out to the store purchase more baking powder, try this replacement. For each teaspoon of baking powder called for in your recipe you can substitute a mixture of: ¼ teaspoon baking soda, ½ teaspoon cream of tartar and ¼ teaspoon cornstarch.

BANANA PRESERVATION

If you will not be able to use those bananas within a day or two, put them into the refrigerator. They will turn black and ugly on the outside, but inside—even after seven to ten days—they will be as fresh and firm as new. This is a great example of when not to let yourself be fooled by outside appearances.

BLENDED "CHEAPUCCINO"

To create a nice version of a blended coffee drink at home, make a very strong pot of coffee (use twice the grinds that you would for regular brew); Pour the hot brewed coffee into ice cube trays and freeze; Pop the frozen cubes into a plastic freezer bag, and return to the freezer. Then, when in need of a treat, place 7 cubes, 1 cup of milk, and 2 ounces of flavoring—plus sugar or sweetener to taste (optional)—in the blender, and puree until smooth for a great drink. Garnish with whipped cream if desired. During the summer months, be sure to keep bags of coffee cubes on hand.

BROWNIE SECRET

Here's the secret to making bakery-quality brownies at home for just pennies. Buy generic or store brand brownie mix and substitute olive oil for the required vegetable oil.

The brownies taste better than those from the fancy bakery uptown. Cheap brownie mix almost always costs less than purchasing the ingredients individually to make from scratch.

BROWN SUGAR SURROGATE

Brown sugar can be replaced with 1 cup of white sugar and 1-to-2 tablespoons of molasses, depending on if you want light or dark brown sugar. Mix thoroughly with a fork. This is so much better than commercial brown sugar that you'll be tempted to make a permanent switch and never again deal with hard brown sugar.

CAKE MIX COOKIES

You can make cookies from any flavor of boxed cake mix. Just add ½ cup of oil, 2 eggs, 1 tablespoon water, and 1 to 2 teaspoons of any flavor of extract to an 18 ounce box of cake mix. Mix well with an electric mixer, roll into 1-inch balls, flatten onto an ungreased cookie sheet, and bake for

8-10 minutes at *350°* F. Get creative with the flavor choices, such as two teaspoons lemon extract with a yellow cake mix for Lemon Cookies. When cooled, dust them with powdered sugar. You can also add 2 teaspoons of vanilla extract to a white cake mix for a delicious sugar cookie; Two teaspoons of mint extract and a chocolate cake mix; white chocolate chips to a strawberry cake mix for a unique result. Get your cake mixes on sale and you cannot beat the price of these cookies. This cookie dough, once mixed, can be frozen for baking later. Just roll into a "log," cover tightly with plastic wrap, and then slice what you need and bake.

CHEESE SAVER

Put a teaspoon of sugar into the bottom of the zip-type plastic bag in which you store cheese. Leave the cheese in its original wrap and make sure you close the bag tightly each time you return it to the refrigerator. You can keep cheese up to 10 weeks this way without any visible evidence of mold.

CINNAMON COFFEE

You can spend a lot on fancy flavored coffee, or you can make your own. Break up a cinnamon stick in coffee grounds before brewing. That's it. Now you can use ordinary supermarket variety coffee, and no one will be the wiser. Beats paying $10 a pound for gourmet cinnamon coffee beans.

CHOCOLATE CHIP STAND-IN

Out of semi-sweet chocolate chips? No problem. In place of 6 ounces of semi-sweet chocolate chips, substitute 9 tablespoons of cocoa, 7 tablespoons of sugar, and 3 tablespoons of butter.

COFFEE STRETCHER

Company is coming, and you're nearly out of coffee. Make this cafe mocha, and you can serve six people with just 2 cups of brewed coffee. Add ⅓ cup cocoa and 3 cups warmed milk to 2 cups of coffee. Sweeten to taste.

COKE MARINADE

Tenderize steaks and cheaper cuts of meat by marinating them in Cola. Several hours ahead of time place the steaks in a bowl and cover them with Cola. Add 2 tablespoons of soy sauce and 1 teaspoon garlic powder. While grilling brush the Cola marinade over the steaks. This is a great way to use up Cola that has gone flat.

CRACKER CRUMB CREATION

Don't throw away broken crackers; instead, use them to make a great salad topping. Crumble ½ slice of bread and mix ¼ cup broken crackers to make perfect breadcrumbs.

FAKE EGG

Short on eggs? No problem. For each egg that you do not have on hand for a recipe, combine two tablespoons of water, two tablespoons of flour and ½ teaspoon of baking powder.

QUICK FAT REMOVAL

No time to refrigerate and wait for fat to harden so it can be removed? Pour the broth into a plastic zipper bag, allow the fat to rise to the top, and then poke a hole in one of the bottom corners. The clear broth strains through the hole.

GINGER FRESH

I have a suggestion for keeping ginger fresh for a long time. Put the ginger into a small container and store it in the freezer. Ginger peels and grates easily when frozen. Use needed amount and return the remainder to the freezer.

FREEZER SOUP

After every meal place whatever vegetables are left over into a bag in the freezer (even if it is just a few corn kernels or green beans). When the bag is full it's time to make soup. Just follow your favorite soup broth/stock recipe. Add leftover beef or chicken and all of those vegetables. This amounts to a free meal as it's all of the scraps you might otherwise have fed to the garbage disposal.

FRESHNESS EXTENDED

Place a piece of plastic wrap directly on top of the sour cream or cottage cheese and press out all of the air space. Now place the lid on top, thus eliminating any air space. This works great on any leftovers, too. It's the exposure to air that encourages bacteria growth.

FROZEN PEPPERS

When they're on sale, stock up on bell peppers. Cut them open, remove the seeds and freeze them in a container with a tight lid. They're better than frozen bell peppers from the store, and much cheaper.

FROZEN WHIPPED CREAM

Fill a waxed milk carton with whipped cream and freeze. When you need some, cut the required amount off the top with a carving knife (carton and all). Recap the carton with plastic wrap or foil, secure with tape or a rubber band and return to the freezer.

GRATED BUTTER

When a recipe says to "dot with butter," instead of cutting a stick of butter into small pieces, grab the cheese grater and "grate" the butter over the large holes right into the casserole, fruit pie or other baked dessert. This will make your butter last longer. Make sure the butter is cold.

GOURMET COFFEE

Do you have a passion for gourmet coffee but don't like to pay the price? Buy coffee on sale and add a sprinkle of cinnamon plus a splash of vanilla and half and half to your hot cup of java. This is much cheaper than your favorite brand of gourmet coffee, which runs about $10 a pound.

GROW SOME YOGURT

Make your own yogurt. Boil ½ gallon of milk and allow it to sit in a cool place. When lukewarm, add 1 tablespoon Dannon plain yogurt, stir, and cover. Let it sit on top of the stove overnight. It will be ready the following day. This mixture will be sugar-free. You can add fruit, honey, or granola to sweeten.

HAM-BONE BENEFITS

What to do with that beautiful holiday ham bone? Freeze
it, and then on a day that's good for making soup, prepare
four pots containing different types of beans and season-
ings. As all four pots simmer, put the bone into one pan at
a time, allowing it to cook for about 20 minutes. Then
move the bone to the next pot and keep the 20-minute rota-
tion going until all four pots of ham and beans are complete. A single bone is more than enough to give wonderful
flavor to all four pots. When the soups are finished, freeze
them into meal-sized portions. It makes a lot!

HANDY BROTH CUBES

If you cook whole chickens for various dishes, you'll end
up with lots of chicken broth. Instead of freezing it in a
large container, fill muffin tins with the broth, freeze, and
then pop into a freezer bag. Now you have homemade
chicken broth in ½ cup portions that you can take from

the freezer as needed. You'll never have to resort to canned broth again.

SUBSTITUTE BUTTERMILK

No buttermilk? Combine 1 cup of fresh milk and 1 table-spoon vinegar for each cup of buttermilk required. Recipes are just guidelines anyway, right?

QUICK CHOCOLATE MOUSSE

So that you are prepared for an unscheduled chocolate fix, learn this substitute: Stir sifted cocoa powder into any tub of any variety Cool Whip. Now taste. Unbelievable, huh?

LEFTOVER MAGICIAN

Want to get your family to eat leftovers? Disguise them as something "new and fresh." For example, chop-up leftover chicken, steak, pork, or hamburger and add it to cheese omelets. Or mix it into Marinara sauce served over pasta, or stir it into rice.

MAKIN' BACON

Next time you buy bacon, come home and cook the entire package. Freeze the cooked pieces individually, two or three in plastic sandwich bags, and when you want bacon just pop it in the microwave for a few seconds for hot sizzling strips.

MEAT TENDERIZER

Use the acidity of vinegar to tenderize meat. Add 2 to 3 tablespoons to pot roast, soups, and stews. If you have balsamic vinegar, it will add a wonderful flavor, but white vinegar tenderizes just as well. Your guests will think you are serving them filet mignon.

MILK CUBES

If you like to use canned milk in your mashed potatoes and coleslaw dressing, you know you never use a full can in the recipe. Invariably, the rest of the can often sours before it can be used. Pour the rest of the can into an ice cube tray and freeze it. Store the cubes in a freezer bag. Now you can take out as many cubes as needed.

SWEET MILK

To make the equivalent of a 14-ounce can of sweetened condensed milk, pour $\frac{1}{2}$ cup of boiling water into a blender; add 1 cup nonfat dry milk, $\frac{2}{3}$ cup sugar, 3 tablespoons of melted butter, and a few drops of vanilla extract. Cover and blend on high speed for 30 seconds or until smooth. Use immediately or store in the refrigerator in a covered container.

EGG REDUCTION

Most cake mixes require 3 eggs, oil, and water. You'll have great results using just the water and 2 eggs. You don't even have to add applesauce (sometimes used as a substitute for eggs or oil in baking). Just set your timer for 2 to 5 minutes less than the package directions. You won't have a dry cake, and this way you save money, calories and cholesterol.

NOODLE KNOW-HOW

Prepackaged meal kits can come in handy for families on those busy evenings, but their portions are too small for many families. Cook 2 or 3 packages of ramen, then stir the noodles into the meal kit. This really fills up a family. A great way to stretch the meal for only about 20 cents!

OVEN-FRIED BACON

Cooking bacon in the oven is so much easier than frying it on the stovetop. The strips cook more consistently and allow more time for other food preparation. No need to babysit the bacon. Use a large rimmed baking sheet, like a jellyroll pan (this will be shallow enough so the bacon cooks, but with the sides high enough to keep in the grease), lined with foil. Preheat oven to *400*° F. Place on the middle rack of the oven for 5 to 6 minutes and then rotate the pan front to back. Continue cooking until bacon is crisp and brown; another 5 to 6 minutes for thin-sliced bacon and 8 to 10 minutes for thick-sliced. Drain, serve, and enjoy!

PERFECT MEATBALLS

When making a large batch of meatballs, the fast and simple way is to shape the meat mixture into a log and cut off slices. The slices roll easily into balls. Another option is to pat the meat into a large square and cut it into cubes which again easily roll into meatballs of uniform size.

YOGURT SUBSTITUTE

Have a craving for yogurt? Don't sweat it. Cottage cheese blended until smooth makes an excellent cup-for-cup substitute for plain yogurt.

HANDY MILK

Store powdered milk in a large container, like Tupperware. You'll find that you will use a lot more powdered milk in cooking when you can easily put the extra product right back in the container.

PUMPKIN PUREE

Here's an easy way to transform an uncooked pumpkin into puree for baking. Select a small, dark orange sugar pumpkin. (Big pumpkins are too stringy for baking.) Cut the pumpkin in half, discard the stringy insides. Microwave on high for 7 minutes per pound. Once cooled, scoop out the flesh, and puree in a food processor, mash with a potato masher, or force through a potato ricer. It's just that easy! You can refrigerate fresh pumpkin puree for up to 3 days and store it in the freezer up to 6 months. This will allow you to enjoy the great taste of fall pumpkins well into the winter.

PUMPKIN SEEDS

Toasted pumpkin seeds make a great snack. Separate the seeds from the stringy membranes that surround them. Rinse and spread on a baking sheet; coat with non-stick spray and sprinkle with a small amount of soy sauce or salt, to taste. Bake at *300°* F for 45 minutes, or until the seeds are golden brown and crunchy. Store in an airtight container.

RECYCLED SPUDS

When peeling potatoes for mashed potatoes save the peelings. Toss them in a bowl, season with salt, pepper and a little Italian dressing and bake at *400°* F for 20 minutes, or until they are crispy, for a quick and healthy snack.

SECRET INGREDIENT

You don't always need top cuts to make a first-rate tasty dish. When making beef stew using a cheaper cut of beef, for example, add a little sweet pickle juice to the mix. The vinegar tenderizes the meat and the juice itself adds great flavor.

SELF-GRATING CHEESE

If you need a large amount of grated cheese, don't waste money on the prepackaged kind. Instead, freeze a block of cheese, thaw it, and it will crumble. You won't waste money, and you won't waste time grating it.

SHORTCUT SPUDS

Potatoes are best when baked in the oven, but that can take up to an hour, heats up the kitchen, and uses lots of energy. To get the speed of the microwave and the wonderful crisp skin of oven-baked, microwave the potatoes until almost done (about 10 minutes in an 1100-watt microwave oven), then transfer them to the toaster oven set at *400°* F for 7 to 10 minutes to finish.

SPINACH SPICE-UP

Keep a bag of frozen chopped spinach in the freezer. Add a handful to spaghetti sauce, ground beef, pizza sauce, fettuccine, etc. Tell the kids the spinach is herbs. They'll eat it up as long as you're careful not to overdo it. They'll actually miss the "herbs" when you forget.

STAND-UP CHICKEN

To roast a whole chicken evenly and more quickly, set your Bundt pan on a cookie sheet. Now stand that chicken over the center cone of the Bundt pan. Roast as you do usually or at 375° F until done. A standing chicken browns more evenly and cooks faster.

SUGARED FRUIT

To make beautiful "sugared fruit" for holiday arrangements and centerpieces, select fruit that is firm and at room temperature (grapes, apples, lemons, etc.). With a pastry brush apply a thin coat of slightly beaten egg white to the fruit. Sprinkle with sugar to cover the entire surface. Dry on a wire rack at least 1 hour before assembling. Display in a glass bowl, pedestal or decorative plate, add ribbon and holiday greens to accent.

SUPER FAST, SUPER FINE

Instead of paying higher prices for the superfine sugar called for in many fancy recipes or for iced tea, grind regular sugar in a blender until super-fine in texture. Keep an eye on it or you will end up with powdered sugar. And that's a tip for making powdered sugar.

THICKEN GRAVY

If you're out of flour, you can substitute pancake mix up to 3 tablespoons. It works well, just don't go over three tablespoons or your guests will be looking for the maple syrup.

TONED-DOWN TOMATO SAUCE

If your homemade tomato sauce is particularly acidic, add a pinch of baking soda. It will fizz at first, but continue to stir it, and the result is a much sweeter sauce with less acid. This helps for those who can get heartburn from tomato sauce.

WINE COOK-ALIKES

To substitute for white cooking wine use ⅓ cup white
grape juice plus 1 tablespoon unseasoned rice vinegar. For
red cooking wine: 1 cup grape juice, 1 tablespoon strong
tea, 1 tablespoon unseasoned rice vinegar.

GARAGE AND PATIO

Many indoor storage solutions and outdoor cleaning agents can be rather expensive, especially when compared to *Everyday Cheapskate* alternatives. Here are some of my favorite cleaning tips and storage solutions for the garage and patio that will give you the results you need without the costs you don't.

CONTENTS—GARAGE AND PATIO

111	Barbecue Cover
111	Charcoal Recycle
111	Storage Buckets
112	Concrete Spot-Remover
112	More Concrete Stains
113	Easy Grill Cleaning
113	Egg Carton Fire Starter
113	Prolong Wicker's Life

BARBECUE COVER

Protect your grill without sacrificing your wallet. Fold an old vinyl tablecloth in half and sew up the sides to make a cover for your outdoor barbecue grill.

CHARCOAL RECYCLE

After the food has cooked on the barbecue, don't leave the coals to just burn out. With a shovel scoop them up into an empty can and smother them by placing a non-flammable lid over the can. They can be used again.

STORAGE BUCKETS

Are you sick of all the half-full bags of fertilizer, potting soil, cat litter, and pet food in the garage that get wet and turn into soggy messes? Go to your local grocery store and ask the bakery for their empty frosting buckets with lids. They are happy to give them away. Just clean them, remove the labels, and make new laminated labels or print clearly on the bucket. This will save you from having to throw out half-full bags of ruined fertilizer or dog food.

CONCRETE SPOT-REMOVER

To clean spots on concrete, sprayed bleach (preferably Clorox) works great. Let it sit for about five minutes; then rinse. Remember to exercise extreme caution when handling liquid chlorine bleach. Do not mix it with anything but water to avoid mixing up a batch of deadly chlorine gas.

MORE CONCRETE STAINS

Commercial cleansers such as Ajax and Comet work well to clean concrete that has been stained by mold or leaves. Sprinkle cleanser on the cement, add water, and scrub with a stiff broom. Allow to sit for a few hours; then rinse.

EASY GRILL CLEANING

Instead of scrubbing your grill clean and making a huge mess, put the grill racks in your self-cleaning oven the next time you run the cycle. The chrome will discolor a little, but you won't spend all that time scrubbing.

EGG CARTON FIRE STARTER

Here's an inexpensive fire starter for a barbecue or camp-fire: Fill an empty paper egg carton with a dozen charcoal briquettes, one in each compartment. Squirt each briquette with lighter fluid, close the fluid container, and then close the egg carton lid. Carefully light the container.

PROLONG WICKER'S LIFE

The life of wicker patio furniture, baskets, or other wicker items can be extended by using salt. To prevent yellowing, scrub wicker furniture with a stiff brush moistened with warm salt water and allow to dry in the sun.

GIFTS

When shopping for gifts, even a cheapskate finds it hard to skimp. And why should you? Your family and friends deserve the best. So go for it in the gift-buying department; just don't go overboard on costs for wrapping those gifts! After all, quality gift-wrap, gift boxes, and all the trimmings can get pretty expensive. Here are some clever, artful, and simple-to-execute tips for making the presentation of your presents ultimately more exciting and eminently cheaper than traditional techniques.

CONTENTS—GIFTS

117	Captain Gift
117	Contractor's Gift Wrap
118	Egg Crate Packing Material
118	Creative Calendar
119	Creative Containers
119	Creative Gift Boxes
120	Draw Names Early
120	Glue Your Gift Wrap
120	Grocery Bags
121	Leftover Lesson
121	Magazine Pages
122	Newspaper Gift Wrap
122	Priceless Gifts
123	Recycled Gift Wraps
123	Road Maps
124	Wrapping "Paper"

CAPTAIN GIFT

Save money by carefully opening cereal boxes, and then reusing them for gift packages. This is extremely popular for kids' gifts. Be aware that your kids might be disappointed when they discover the gift inside isn't cereal after all.

CONTRACTOR'S GIFT WRAP

Your gift can be the hit of the party when it's wrapped with authentic drywall, screws, and joint compound—then tied with joint tape. Unwrapping this can be the best entertainment of the night. While this might be a bit extreme, it's a good reminder to let your imagination run wild. The secret is to capitalize on the uniqueness of your wrap, not try to disguise or hide what it really is. Why not? It's all going to land in the trash anyway, so you might as well have fun.

EGG CRATE PACKING MATERIAL

Save clean foam egg cartons and use the egg holder side as padding for mailing gifts and packages. Cut off and discard the lids and then cut the egg holder side to fit the space. They are easy to store because they nest, take up less space than packing "peanuts," and work better than any other packing material. No one likes to spend money on bubble wrap.

CREATIVE CALENDAR

For parents who collect hundreds of artwork papers every school year and hate to throw them out, here's an excellent gift suggestion: Start collecting next year's calendars from local businesses. Select 12 of the most precious pieces of your child's artwork for each calendar and affix them over the printed calendar pictures. Rubber cement gives a good result. This makes a practical gift that is even more special because of the sentiment. Grandparents, godparents, aunts, and uncles are always delighted, the child is ecstatic, and the cost is minimal. Finish off the calendar by attaching the child's photograph and signature.

CREATIVE CONTAINERS

Decorative tins, baskets, flower pots, glass jars, decorated oatmeal canisters, or coffee cans can all become unique wraps for gifts. Plus, all the different sizes and shapes of these decorative containers give you lots of options for finding your gift a perfect match.

CREATIVE GIFT BOXES

To avoid spending money on gift boxes, recycle food storage boxes such as cereal, Jell-O, and cracker boxes. Just break open the box at the seam, turn it inside out and then tape or glue it back together. Your family members get a big kick out of discovering what type of box you used for their gift. It makes Christmas time more interesting, too, because the boxes are so many different shapes and sizes.

DRAW NAMES EARLY

Many families draw names for their annual Christmas gift exchange. If so, do the drawing as soon as all the gifts are opened on Christmas morning. That means you'll have 12 months to find the perfect gifts at a discount. If the grandparents aren't involved in the exchange, they can hold the master copy in case someone forgets the name they drew.

GLUE YOUR GIFT WRAP

When wrapping a lot of presents, taping can be such a pain. Instead of using tape to seal your gift wrap, keep a glue stick handy for sealing packages. Costs less, dries fast, and gives your gifts that professional "no-tape" look.

GROCERY BAGS

Cut open a brown grocery bag and you have an unprinted piece of very heavy Kraft paper, perfect for gift wrapping. You can rubber stamp the paper, or leave plain and top with a plaid ribbon. Idea: Tear strips of fabric (homespun is ideal) for ribbon. Use with the Kraft paper for a beautiful country look.

LEFTOVER LESSON

Leftover wallpaper or shelf paper can find a new purpose as unique gift wrap. Keep your eyes open for large sheets of paper from work such as architectural drawings or blueprints that are headed for the trash.

MAGAZINE PAGES

Many of the pages in a high-quality magazine have no text, only beautiful graphics. A single page from *Martha Stewart Living* or *O* Magazine is the perfect size to wrap a CD, DVD, or other small item. Tape several pages together for a larger gift.

NEWSPAPER GIFT WRAP

The Sunday comics make excellent gift wrap, especially for kids. Here's another great idea: Find a page that is mostly "gray space" with no large ads or pictures, such as the bland stock market listings. Get out your rubber stamps (large foam stamps work especially well), and go to work. Stamp randomly using a red or green stamp pad for an overall design. You'll be amazed at how good this looks.

PRICELESS GIFTS

If you enjoy genealogy as a hobby, a notebook of family history and important information (and photos if you have a scanner) makes a great gift for Christmas or a wedding, especially if you have access to both the bride's and groom's information. This history can be as simple or as elaborate as your time and finances allow.

RECYCLED GIFT WRAPS

It makes a lot of sense to carefully unwrap gifts, rescue the paper, and save it for later. But that tedious routine can annoy the people around you. Having said that, here are a couple of tips for how to re-use gift wrap so no one is the wiser. To remove folds and wrinkles from gift wrap paper, lightly spray the wrong side with spray starch and iron it out using the low and dry settings on your iron. Roll onto a cardboard tube to store.

ROAD MAPS

Pair the travelers on your list with those maps that are just taking up space and use them as gift wrap. Outline the route of a past trip or one you hope to take one day. Add funny notes or whimsical sayings that pertain to the different points of interest.

WRAPPING "PAPER"

Use a kitchen or bath towel as the wrapping "paper" for a bridal or shower gift. Use a ribbon or yarn to decorate the package, add a great family recipe on a recipe card as the gift tag and some useful utensil as the bow. All the useful wrapping becomes part of the gift.

GROCERY SHOPPING

There are lots of ways to save money on food shopping besides clipping coupons and skimping on quality with no-frills products. And if you're willing to decrease your dining-out experiences, your family can eat like kings on a smart budget with a little ingenuity at the store and at home. From freezer tricks and cyber shopping to seeking super sales and corresponding with your favorite food companies, the clever tips in this chapter will help save you lots of money without sacrificing quality.

CONTENTS—GROCERY SHOPPING

129	Bakery Items
129	Early Bird
129	Clip Coupons
130	Constructive Complaining
130	Scanner Sleuth
131	Mealtime Math
131	Make-A-Wish
132	Clipper Kids
132	Coupon Give Away
133	Coupon Savings
133	Cyber List
134	Deli Dash
134	Frozen Concentrate
134	Hungry Shopper Alert
135	Load up on Loss Leaders
135	Milk a Discount
136	Store-Brand
136	Grocery Gift Card
136	Switch Neighborhoods
137	Pro Store Brand
137	Rethink

BAKERY ITEMS

Find a bakery outlet (check the phone book) where bakeries unload the day's overproduction. You'll discover high-quality, fresh products at rock-bottom prices. Time your trip for Sale Day and save 50 percent or more! Bakery items freeze well, so stock up.

EARLY BIRD

Supermarket meat managers chop as much as 50 percent from the original price of meat, fish, and poultry when expiration dates are near. Make friends with the store personnel so you'll be first in line to grab the bounty. Items close to the expiration date not consumed within 24 hours should be frozen.

CLIP COUPONS

Too much work for little pay-off? Expert Teri Gault (www.thegrocerygame.com) says you don't have to be a world-class "couponer" to realize significant savings. Anyone can clip 15 percent from the grocery bill with only a minimal effort. Always select the smallest size a coupon allows to reap the greatest savings.

CONSTRUCTIVE COMPLAINING

Write a concise note to manufacturers like Pepperidge Farm or Nabisco and tell them what you really like or really don't like about a specific product. You will find an address for customer service on the product. It's likely that companies will send you coupons, which is a great return on a stamp and a few minutes of your time.

SCANNER SLEUTH

Many supermarkets have a policy that if an item scans differently from the shelf price, it's free. Do your shopping early in the day after the price changes. Find out when your store changes their specials and prices. You can be the first shopper to discover the problems, and you'll benefit from it. The store is grateful when customers help them catch their mistakes. You can save so much money by just knowing your prices and keeping your eye on the scanner. It all adds up.

MEALTIME MATH

Figure out how much it costs per meal to eat at home by dividing your monthly grocery bill by the number of meals and then by the number of people in your household. You may think twice next time you want to eat out.

MAKE-A-WISH

Do you go shopping when you're feeling blue? Even if you're trying to spend less, you still have to shop. So, just take along a small notepad with you instead of cash and make a wish list. When you get home, your blues will be gone and you can make plans to save for these items on your list. Once you have saved for them, you might find you can live without them and then have a little extra cash to use for something more important.

CLIPPER KIDS

A great way to teach children how to save money is to offer them a deal: If they would like to be in charge of clipping grocery store coupons and keeping them organized (and accompanying you to the store, of course), they are entitled to keep the savings. They will quickly learn how unimportant brand loyalty is.

COUPON GIVE AWAY

Here's a perfect use for unwanted or expired manufacturer's coupons. Mail them to military families stationed abroad who can use them at the base commissary, up to six months after they expire. Military families are really struggling to make ends meet, especially those with several children. Go to www.siteforsavings.com and click on "Send Coupons to Service Families" for details.

COUPON SAVINGS

If you're trying to save for something special and often use grocery store coupons, try this: When checking out at the grocery store, ask the cashier for a subtotal. Write the check for that amount, then have the coupons credited and receive cash back for the savings. Put that extra money in an envelope or special account to save for that item you've been wanting. You will learn that it adds up quickly.

CYBER LIST

Check your grocery store's website for weekly specials. You can browse through the week's specials and sales that are applicable to your zip code at your store's website. Some sites allow you to add the specials along with other items onto you online shopping list, print it out, and head to the store.

DELI DASH

If you shop at a Wal-Mart SuperCenter, head to the deli at 9 P.M. That's when they usually sell the hot deli foods and whole roasted chickens for half price. Rotisserie chicken for $2 is a bargain when whole fryers in the meat counter can cost up to $5.

FROZEN CONCENTRATE

If the mixing instructions say 3 cans of water, add 4. Frozen juice is so highly concentrated a little extra water won't make a taste difference, but you'll immediately reduce your juice cost by 25 percent.

HUNGRY SHOPPER ALERT

Grocery store checkers are right when they recommend never shop when you are hungry. Checkers can easily pick the hungry shoppers from the rest. Not only do they buy more stuff when they arrive hungry, their carts are full of junk food. If you can't eat before you get to the store, grab a roll or cookie from the bakery before you start your shopping.

LOAD UP ON LOSS LEADERS

Watch the grocery, discount, and retail store ads and buy loss leader and sale items. The goal is to never run out of any item that you use so you are not forced to buy at full price. Buying things only when they are on sale takes extra planning and storage space, but the savings make it worth the effort.

MILK A DISCOUNT

With milk prices sky high, buying at a discount makes more sense than ever. Save at least $1 gallon at a warehouse club. Low-fat milk freezes well so stock up if space permits.

STORE-BRAND

Wal-Mart powdered automatic dishwasher detergent is about the best buy for the buck. Many Cascade fans find this particular store brand to be superior even to their highly regarded Cascade brand.

GROCERY GIFT CARD

Once a month, buy a cash card from your supermarket for the amount you've budgeted on groceries for the month. As you shop during the month, pay with the card. Seeing that decreasing balance will help you keep track of where you are in your spending for the month. It will also keep you from spending the grocery money for other things, because the card is only good at that chain.

SWITCH NEIGHBORHOODS

The prices in two supermarkets owned by the same company can vary by as much as 10 percent when one is located in an upscale community, the other in a lower-income area. Patronize the lower-priced store and reap the savings.

PRO STORE BRAND

These days, generic and store brands are often the same as the national brand, only the label and price (which reflects built-in advertising costs) are different. Make the switch and enjoy the savings. Are you disappointed with a store brand item? Take advantage of the store's satisfaction guaranteed policy and return it for a refund.

RETHINK

Do not be too much of a cheapskate in the supermarket. Eating out, even at a fast-food restaurant, costs far more than food made at home. So paying an extra dollar for your favorite bread, buying quality meat and cheese, and picking up a few treats in the supermarket will save you money, if it means you won't be tempted to eat out. Burgers made at home cost less and are healthier than at the drive-thru.

HEALTH AND BEAUTY

Whether you want to look good or just to feel better, reaching your goal traditionally comes at a significant cost. But not if you're a dedicated cheapskate! While medications and beauty products you use must be safe, there's no reason that you have to pay exorbitant prices to ensure such quality. Here are some fascinating and functional tips for saving time and stretching costs on everything from razor blades to body soap to prescription drugs to dandruff shampoo and more.

CONTENTS—HEALTH AND BEAUTY

142	Elder Wipes
142	Cash for Generic
143	Dandruff Solution
143	Eye Make-Up Remover
144	Hot Tick Trick
144	Finger Shrink
144	Half-Price Hair Color
145	Hot Oil Treatment
145	Medicine Location
146	Prescription Assistance
147	Prescription Possibilities
147	Prolong Blade Life
148	Recycle Old Glasses
148	Rock Bottom Prices
148	Salon-Style Hair Treatment
149	Shorten Make-Up Pencils
149	Snip and Save
150	Message Mirror
150	Soap Sliver Solution
150	Softer Skin
151	Split Pills

151   Tonic for Tobacco Teeth

152   Shower Solution

153   Student Health Services

ELDER WIPES

Here's a wonderful alternative to the normal soap and water solution when giving bed baths to elderly or patients on bed rest. Mix 4 cups of warm water, 4 tablespoons of mineral oil, and 2 tablespoons Johnson's baby body wash. Pour some into a wash basin and use with clean wash-cloths. Rinsing is not necessary.

CASH FOR GENERIC

It is often less expensive to pay outright for your generic prescriptions, as if you did not have health insurance. The co-pay for a generic prescription is generally $10. But the cash price at many pharmacies for a 90-day supply of that medication is more like $18, or just $6 per month. Of course the pharmacy doesn't volunteer this information; you'll have to find it out on your own. Two things you need to know: How your medications are classified and how much your co-pay is for that classification. Then you need to shop around. Call several pharmacies to learn their cash price, and then ask your doctor to write your prescriptions for 90 days at a time.

DANDRUFF SOLUTION

To control occasional dandruff, add one drop of peppermint oil for every 2 ounces of shampoo and shake well before using. Don't add more oil, as it will burn like fire if you add too much. The peppermint oil will give a wonderful smell and a crisp, clean feel to the hair and scalp. A bottle of the essential oil costs about $6-$7 and lasts for years when using one drop at a time. Added to an economy brand, this makes it the equivalent of Paul Mitchell or Tea Tree shampoos for just a few more pennies per bottle.

EYE MAKE-UP REMOVER

Use a no-tears type baby shampoo to remove eye make-up. Ophthalmologists encourage contact lens wearers to do this to reduce protein build-up on their lenses. It works great. No stinging because it is, after all, no tears; and it's cheap.

HOT TICK TRICK

The best, easiest and safest way to remove a tick that has already bitten and burrowed itself is to douse it with Tabasco sauce. The tick will pull out in seconds. It really works!

FINGER SHRINK

If you've had a ring stuck on a swollen finger, here's a great tip: Rub Preparation-H on your finger to temporarily reduce the swelling enough to get the ring off. It's painless, quick and might save you a trip to the jeweler to have the ring cut off.

HALF-PRICE HAIR COLOR

Make a single-use hair-coloring kit stretch into two applications. Instead of mixing all of the product and throwing away part because it's more than you need, pour half of the solution into a bowl and mix it with half of the developer in the other bottle. Cap the bottles for the next time. Once mixed, it must be used; this is why you need to be careful to mix only half of each bottle.

HOT OIL TREATMENT

To give your hair a treat, try this hot oil treatment: Wet hair thoroughly under hot water (as hot as you can stand), then apply up to one tablespoon, depending on hair length, of generic baby oil, making sure you completely saturate the ends. Wrap hair in a towel and leave for at least 30 minutes (longer is better for long hair). Rinse, then shampoo, and condition as usual. You can do this for a fraction of the cost of a salon or commercial hot oil treatment.

MEDICINE LOCATION

The worst place for a medicine cabinet is in the bathroom. Most medications deteriorate in a bathroom's warm, moist environment. They keep much better in a cool, dry place like a linen closet, on a high shelf that is out of the reach of children.

PRESCRIPTION ASSISTANCE

Most pharmaceutical companies have a Patient Assistance program whereby they ship free prescription drugs either to your door or to your doctor's office, if you are uninsured or underinsured. Most have an income limit of $16,000 to $18,000, for single households, and $24,000 for two or more. Find the toll-free number of the drug's manufacturer (ask your pharmacist if you do not know) and ask to speak with Patient Assistance. You'll get right through. You will have to complete forms and submit them to your doctor, but you'll find most companies to be courteous and eager to help those who qualify.

PRESCRIPTION POSSIBILITIES

Most physicians are generously supplied with medication samples (also known as "stock bottles") by pharmaceutical companies. Always ask for a supply of these samples when your doctor prescribes medication. It is very frustrating to spend a fortune on an expensive prescription only to find out you're allergic to it or it is not effective. Trying a sample first can prevent a big, expensive mistake.

PROLONG BLADE LIFE

Disposable razor blades get dull quickly because the metal blades begin to oxidize from the first time they touch water. They will last almost twice as long if you can slow down that process. Rinse razors well after use and store them blade head down in a small cup of cooking oil. Light canola oil works best.

RECYCLE OLD GLASSES

Getting new glasses can be expensive, but it doesn't have to be. When you purchase new eyeglasses, keep your old frames. If the prescription has only changed slightly, get the lenses tinted and use them as sunglasses.

ROCK BOTTOM PRICES

Costco and Sam's Club offer deeply discounted prices on prescription drugs. Compare pricing with Eckerd Drugs, Walgreens, and CVS. While Costco's price is substantially cheaper, Sam's Club has a policy to meet or beat Costco's prices.

SALON-STYLE HAIR TREATMENT

Hair stylists recommend this cheap home treatment instead of an expensive $25 or $35 salon treatment for removing build-up of minerals, conditioners, sprays, mousses, and gels. Wash hair with a gentle shampoo and rinse in cool water. Towel dry hair. Saturate hair with apple cider vinegar (not white vinegar which is too harsh). Do not rinse yet, but instead wrap hair in a plastic cap or plastic wrap and heat with a blow dryer for 10 to 15 minutes. Rinse hair thoroughly and shampoo again.

SHORTEN MAKE-UP PENCILS

Long lip liner and eyeliner pencils are awkward and don't fit into the typical make-up bag. Solution: Break one in half, sharpen both pieces. Now you have two manageable pencils for the price of one.

SNIP AND SAVE

Facial cleansing cloths have become popular and very handy. They come dry and when you wet them they suds up. The cloths are too large for a single use, but are not reusable. Solution: Cut them into halves or quarter. The cost savings is amazing.

Everyday Cheapskate's Greatest Tips

MESSAGE MIRROR

Communicate with your loved ones using an already
installed device. Use dry erase markers to leave messages
for each other on your bathroom mirror. Works great, and
you don't have to add another message board to your
home.

SOAP SLIVER SOLUTION

You will never have to worry about what to do with those
soap slivers again if you do this: When a bar of soap
reduces to between ½ and ⅓ of its original size, simply
lather up another bar and attach it to that one. Once dry
they'll "glue" themselves together. Combine different bars
of soaps for an interesting effect. However, it won't work if
either bar is Dove.

SOFTER SKIN

Fir a quick and cheap facial, mix dry oatmeal and water

into a paste and spread it on your face, avoiding the eyes and nostrils. Lie down and let it dry for about 5 to 10 minutes. Then, wash off gently with warm water. The results are amazing, and the cost is minimal.

SPLIT PILLS

If you take medication, ask your doctor to prescribe a pill that can be split. For example if you take 100 mg twice a day, ask for the 200 mg strength. You can cut it in half, reducing your monthly allotment by half. You'll be surprised to discover that for most medications there is very little difference, if any, between the dosage strengths. You can even buy a "pill splitter" at the pharmacy to make splitting pills a cinch.

TONIC FOR TOBACCO TEETH

Having tobacco stains on your teeth isn't exactly appealing, not to mention your tobacco breath. Here's a recipe for tooth stain remover (similar to Targon Smoker's Mouthwash) for removing coffee, tea and tobacco stains. Mix together in a container that has a lid: 1/2 cup cheap vodka or gin, 2 teaspoons glycerin (check with pharmacist), 4 cups water, 2 teaspoons flavoring (mint is good), a few drops of food coloring (try green), and 3 packets artificial sweetener. Label. Swish through teeth for one minute prior to brushing. Spit out. Brush as usual for two minutes. If used regularly, you will see a difference in about a week. As with all medicinal products, keep out of reach of children. Not particularly toxic, but not good to drink.

SHOWER SOLUTION

Get the most suds for your cents. Shower with White Rain shampoo. This is the best lathering and most economical "shower product," and it works great if you have hard water, too.

STUDENT HEALTH SERVICES

Part of most college student fees goes toward student health services. The service can include unlimited visits with doctors, nurse practitioners and nurses, routine lab work, X-rays, pharmacy, health education, orthopedics, and HIV and STD testing. Low-cost services include travel immunizations, flu shots, discounted prescriptions, and CPR and First Aid classes. Have your college student check out their campus student health services.

HOME

Sometimes *home, sweet home* can seem like a money pit. But your house doesn't have to cost you tons for upkeep when you use ingenuity, creativity, shopping sense, and *savings* sense to bring out the best without breaking the bank. In this chapter, you'll find some sweet and sensible tips—from flowers to art to flooring to postcards to decorating to saving stamps and more—for making your house a wonderful home, with money and time to spare.

CONTENTS—HOME

158	Fragrant Home
158	Unlist on Google
159	Unseal Envelopes
159	Stabilizer Substitute
159	Picture Postcards
160	Recycle Florist Items
160	Drying Flowers
161	Appliance Aptitude
161	Bargain Art
162	Bag the Floor
163	Bag Your Own
163	Bag the Sheets
163	Bathroom Pinup
164	Decorating Details
164	Just Whites
165	Check the Vent
165	Custom Mini Blinds
166	Curtain Tie Back
166	Darken the Fridge
167	Dishwasher Rinse Agent
167	Extra Compaction

168	Fragrant Trash
168	Frugal Fragrance
168	Hard Water Dissolver
169	Houseplant Intensive Care
169	Lights Out
170	Make Your Own Pillowcases
170	More for Less
171	No Ghosts
171	Pillows from Napkins
172	Pinecone Fire Starters
172	Secret Pillows
173	Sleep Under the Stars
173	Stop Smoking Candles
174	Tastefully Trashed
174	Terry Towels are Terrific
175	Vacuum for Small Places
175	Vase Value
176	Whiteboard Wanna-Be
176	Wise Wax Removal

FRAGRANT HOME

To keep the air in your home fragrant during the autumn months cut a length of panty hose, put your favorite spice blend inside, tie both ends and place it just inside a heating vent. Or add some spices to the vacuum cleaner bag. This is a great way to use up kitchen spices that are older than six months and have lost their strength and pungency.

UNLIST ON GOOGLE

Do you want to block Google from divulging your private information? Log on to www.google.com, the Internet search engine. Type your home phone number into the search bar. If your street address and name comes up, click on "map" to get detailed driving directions to your front door. As convenient as this may appear, the safety issues are alarming. If your phone number is unlisted, you should be fine, but check anyway. To unlist, simply click on the telephone icon next to your phone number. You will see a link that allows you to remove yourself.

UNSEAL ENVELOPES

There are times that you need to unseal a letter you've written to either change or add to its contents. Here's a handy way to do that without ruining the envelope: Put it in the freezer for a few hours. Slide a knife under the flap and it will pop open. Even better, the glue is still good so you can reseal it.

STABILIZER SUBSTITUTE

Think you need another set of hands in order to get your sewing done? Try this tip: A paper coffee filter works great as a fabric stabilizer for performing machine embroidery.

PICTURE POSTCARDS

After placing photos in your album and sending some to relatives, take the extra prints and use them for postcards. You'll always have a postcard on hand for contests, quick notes to friends, etc. Plus, instead of becoming trash, they have one more life.

RECYCLE FLORIST ITEMS

Instead of throwing away those empty vases and baskets that held your flowers, or letting them turn into more clutter, ask your florist if they take the containers and baskets back. Many florists not only take them back but will also give you fresh flowers in exchange. It's a nice way to recycle and get something in return.

DRYING FLOWERS

Use plain cheap clay cat litter to dry roses and other flowers. Put a layer of cat litter in the bottom of a box lined with a paper towel. Place your roses so they are not touching each other in the litter. Gently add more litter to cover the flowers. They will be completely dried in about 7 to 10 days. Take them out and shake very gently to remove the excess litter. Spray them with the cheapest super-hold hairspray you can find to seal and protect them. You'll find it will take years to use up that bag of litter. This method works much better than the expensive silica gel sold in craft stores for flower drying.

APPLIANCE APTITUDE

Before calling the appliance repairman, try a few simple steps. Call the local parts distributors in your area and ask them for possible solutions to your appliance problem. Most appliance problems can be correctly diagnosed over the phone and fixed with a little common sense. Always have the correct brand and model in hand when you call as each appliance has individual solutions. Using your own labor to replace parts can save a lot of money.

BARGAIN ART

Wait until after the New Year to get closeout prices on calendars with big splashy prints by wonderful artists. Save the images until you find an appropriate frame and mat. Thrift stores, yard sales, discount stores, or hobby shops are good sources. You can have the most wonderful collection of your favorite artist for just pennies per print.

BAG THE FLOOR

Create a gorgeous floor made from paper grocery bags. Tear the bags into pieces and apply to a level, clean, smooth floor with wallpaper paste (printed side down, if any). When dry, apply stain (golden oak works well). This will be absorbed in varying degrees to produce a leather-like look. Apply multiple coats of polyurethane designed for wood floors, sanding between coats. You'll want to apply at least six coats so it wears beautifully. Install molding around the edges (quarter round works well) to insure the edges stay down. What a gorgeous, yet inexpensive floor.

BAG YOUR OWN

Many towns do not offer garbage pick up as a municipal service so residents can contract with whomever they desire. This service can add up if you are charged by the bag or container. However, if you live in the vicinity of a landfill, many now accept bagged garbage for a minimal charge per bag. And if you recycle, you'll have very little true garbage to be picked up.

BAG THE SHEETS

Store your sheet sets inside their matching pillowcases. Tuck the folded sheets and one pillowcase inside the other case for tidy stacking in the linen closet. No more search-ing for the flat sheet that matches the fitted one you want to use. Everything is neatly tucked inside of its own "bag."

BATHROOM PINUP

Are you tired of towels left on the floor after your child

washes his hands? Hang the towel on a rack and pin the front and back together with a large safety or diaper pin. If you pin it from the back side no one will ever notice and your towel will stay put.

DECORATING DETAILS

When you finish refurbishing a room in your home, write down this important information on a piece of paper and tape it to the back of the switch plate: The brand and color of the paint, how much paint was needed to coat the room; how many rolls of wallpaper were required; and the circuit breaker number that serves this room. You'll be happy to find the information next time you need to re-paint.

JUST WHITES

Fine hotels everywhere feature all white linens. You should, too. When everything is white, you don't worry about fading, about matching up sets or if the linens match the room's decor. Every top sheet goes with every fitted sheet, so you don't have laundry hassles. Everything launders the same. White linens are classic and they're cheaper too. Now everything matches, which saves time and hassle.

CHECK THE VENT

If your clothes dryer is not properly vented, it could be wasting energy. The standard vinyl-coated accordion-type vent restricts the flow of wet air from your dryer. Install a rigid sheet metal vent, and clothes will dry much faster (sometimes twice as fast). The vent sections are available from your local home center. Savings can amount to $100 per year.

CUSTOM MINI BLINDS

If you have windows that are taller than the standard, you don't have to pay for custom blinds. Instead, purchase three blinds that are the correct width. Use sections of the third blind to lengthen the short ones. Following the instructions for how to shorten blinds, remove the bottom portion, tie on the necessary extra blinds and replace the finished bottoms.

CURTAIN TIE BACK

If you like the simplicity and look of curtain "holdbacks" (the decorative hardware that holds curtains to one side) you might be shocked when the least expensive set you find is $12 a pair. Instead, buy the screw hooks that are used to hang a bicycle ($1 for a package of two) and are the same size as holdbacks. These steel hooks are vinyl coated and come in a variety of bright colors—the perfect custom holdbacks that match a child's room, bathroom, or kitchen. You can use hot glue to attach decorative items such as silk flowers, shells, ribbons, buttons—just about anything to bring in the décor and theme of the room.

DARKEN THE FRIDGE

If your kids are constantly in and out of the refrigerator eating the food faster than you can replenish it, remove the light bulb. If they are really hungry, they will take the time to search, otherwise it won't be worth the bother.

DISHWASHER RINSE AGENT

Instead of pricey commercial rinse agents, fill that little reservoir in your dishwasher with white vinegar. Your dishes will sparkle. Refill often. If your dishwasher does not have this feature, simply add ½ cup into the last rinse.

EXTRA COMPACTION

Some models of trash compactors have a switch for extra compaction and you can do the same thing even if yours doesn't have this feature. Start the compactor and just as the motor starts to reverse, turn the switch off. This stops the ram in the bottom position and eliminates the re-expansion of the trash. If you leave yours in this position overnight it doubles the capacity of the bag. Less cost for bags and fewer trips to the dumpster.

FRAGRANT TRASH

I place the scented perfume ads that appear in department store advertisements and magazines at the bottom of small wastebaskets scattered throughout my home. I toss it out when I empty the trash and start again.

FRUGAL FRAGRANCE

Add a couple of drops of your favorite perfume or essential oil to the inside of the cardboard toilet tissue roll. With each turn, fragrance is released into the room.

HARD WATER DISSOLVER

Vinegar will dissolve hard-water marks like those on shower doors, faucets, and in vases. If the vinegar is hot (you can heat it in the microwave), it works faster.

HOUSEPLANT INTENSIVE CARE

If your houseplants don't do well during the winter months, it could be for a lack of humidity. Most homes have about 20 percent humidity during the winter, but houseplants need 40 to 60 percent. You can mist them 2 to 3 times a day, or use a furnace humidifier to get that humidity level up. For plants that appear very sick, give them a very good misting then make a humidity tent by slipping a clear plastic bag over any drooping plant, staking if needed to keep the bag from touching the leaves. Secure the bottom of the bag to the side of the pot with string or rubber bands. The plant should perk up in about a week. Remove the bag and resume normal care. Humidity tents are a good idea if you take a winter vacation, too.

LIGHTS OUT

If it appears your kids don't know "how" to turn the lights off, install mechanical time switches (available at home improvement stores) in strategic places like bathrooms, basement, and the laundry room. They are available in times from 15 minutes to several hours and are easy to install. Once the time expires the lights turn off automatically.

MAKE YOUR OWN PILLOWCASES

Extra pillowcases can be very pricey, so consider making your own: When you buy your next set of sheets, buy an additional flat queen-sized sheet to match, regardless of the size of the matching set. Out of the queen flat sheet you can make three pairs of matching pillowcases for a fraction of the cost of buying them ready made. By measuring a commercially made pillowcase, it is easy to create a usable pattern.

MORE FOR LESS

If you prefer the square facial tissue boxes but hate paying more for fewer tissues (they really do have about half the quantity of the regular box of tissues), reuse an empty square tissue box by carefully opening one side. Remove about half of the tissues from a regular size box. Fold the stack in half and insert it into the square box fold facing up, so you can pull out the tissue through the box's top opening. Tape the side shut till the next refill.

NO GHOSTS

Help your dry-erase markers last longer. Regularly wipe down your whiteboard with liquid car wax applied with a soft cloth. This keeps the markers from "ghosting."

PILLOWS FROM NAPKINS

Make throw pillows from cloth table napkins. Sew (or glue) two napkins, decorative sides facing, together, leaving an opening for stuffing. Turn the decorative sides out. Stuff. Close the opening. For a different effect before turning the decorative side out, wrap a rubber band tightly around each corner. This causes a softer, gathered corner. These pillows turn out lovely.

PINECONE FIRE STARTERS

Place a coffee can in a pan of water on the stove. Melt blocks of paraffin in the coffee can. Add cinnamon, nutmeg, or other scents to the paraffin (you can purchase scented paraffin if you prefer, but it's more expensive). You can also add colored wax or drops of oil to the melted paraffin. Tie a piece of candlewick or string through the top of a pinecone. Dip dried pinecones into the paraffin. Allow paraffin to harden and dip again, allowing paraffin to harden after each dip. These make a great gift. Simply package them in a mesh bag or other packaging and add a tag reading: Place pinecones under logs before lighting.

SECRET PILLOWS

If you love the bed-and-breakfast "cottage" look with lots of throw pillows, here's how you can get that look on a budget: Make simple throw pillow covers with the fabric overlapping on the back side secured with a button. Then, instead of buying costly pillow inserts, neatly fold your winter blankets and slip them inside. This solves the problem of where to store the blankets during the summer months, and provides an abundance of inexpensive and decorative throw pillows. An added bonus is that the covers are very easy to clean. Just remove and toss in the laundry.

SLEEP UNDER THE STARS

Instead of buying glow-in-the-dark plastic stars or stickers for your kids' rooms there's a cheaper way to create the night sky. Dab glow-in-the-dark paint on the tip of a skinny dowel and randomly tap the ceiling. The 'dots' won't show during the day, but at night they glow and even seem to twinkle.

STOP SMOKING CANDLES

Trim candle wicks to one-quarter of an inch. A short wick produces a smaller, more controlled flame that won't emit as much smoke. Snip the excess after each use to get rid of black buildup on the tip, which causes the wick to bend and the wax to melt unevenly. Never leave wick trimmings on the candle, nor leave a room with a candle still lit.

TASTEFULLY TRASHED

Keep a tasteful trash receptacle where you open mail. Don't carry all of the junk mail to the table for it to only become household clutter. Put a waste can right where you open the mail and dump the junk the moment you identify it as such.

TERRY TOWELS ARE TERRIFIC

Don't buy kitchen towels in the housewares department. Instead, go to the automotive department and purchase the white terry cloth towels. A package of 12 in some areas costs under $5, and they don't shed or wear out quickly. They're great in the kitchen and for cleaning around the house, too.

VACUUM FOR SMALL PLACES

If your vacuum cleaner attachments are too large for small tight spaces, attach an ordinary drinking straw to the end of the smallest attachment. First insert about 1/3 of the straw into the attachment and then seal the connection between the two with a piece of tape. Then the straw can fit into small tight spaces (like keyboards) and suck out the dirt. You won't have to purchase a separate machine equipped with small attachments to do the same job.

VASE VALUE

The next time you empty a salad dressing bottle, clean it up and remove the label. Most are the perfect shape to hold a small bouquet of flowers. It will be larger than a bud vase and perfect for when you want to display just a few flowers. Tie a ribbon around the screw threads and no one will be the wiser.

WHITEBOARD WANNA-BE

If you want to hang a whiteboard in a child's room, play-room, or office, but are hesitant to purchase one at the office-supply store (they can be pricey), purchase shower board, sold in 6-foot sheets at building and home supply stores. Cut it to any size you desire. It is a comparable material for a fraction of the price. You can make a simple frame for your board or mount it on the wall unframed.

WISE WAX REMOVAL

Here's an easy way to remove all of the wax and black residue left in candleholders once the candle has burned down. Turn them upside down in a vegetable steamer. Put water in the bottom as you would to steam vegetables, cover and allow to steam for 10 or 15 minutes. The candleholders will be clean and once the water cools, you can simply skim off the hardened wax, which makes it easy to clean the pot.

KITCHEN TRICKS

Here is a wonderfully creative collection of tips that spotlight my readers' resourcefulness and intelligence in the kitchen and pantry. You'll learn how to make the most of your time in the kitchen. From clever tricks involving coffee filters, kitchen mallets, and shower caps (yes, shower caps!), to simple storage solutions for sugars and spices, this chapter takes conventional wisdom to an unconventional level.

CONTENTS—KITCHEN TRICKS

182	Calcium Stretch
182	Cheap Clips
182	No More Flipping
183	Cone Coffee Filters
183	Odor Eliminator
183	Cubed Eggs
184	Easy Defrost
184	Two Loaves, One Loaf Pan
185	No More Ice Crystals
185	Easy Store, Quick Thaw
186	Film Canister Measure
186	Flat Frozen Food
187	Flatware Timesaver
187	Freezer Fill Up
188	Fresh Disposal
188	Fresh Lettuce
188	Fridge Caps
189	Frozen Rice
189	Frugal Luxury
189	Fun with Filters
190	Half-Price Spice

190	Kitchen Mallet
191	Leftover Inventory
191	Newsprint Solution
192	Process with Plastic
192	Refrigerator Reduction
192	Sealed Plastic Bags
193	Soft Sugar
193	Spicy Solution
194	Tie Into A Bow

CALCIUM STRETCH

Add powdered milk to meatloaf, meatballs, and cookie recipes. It is cheap and a good way to add calcium to your diet. Most kids won't touch milk made from powder, but mixed into other foods, they'll have no idea it's there.

CHEAP CLIPS

Need a cheap but effective way to clamp shut your chip bags, etc.? Buy bags of clothespins at the dollar store. They make great chip clips!

NO MORE FLIPPING

Instead of flipping pancakes, bake them. Pour the batter into a lightly oiled jellyroll pan and bake at *400°* F for 20 minutes. Cut them into squares for the adults and use animal shaped cookie cutters for the kids. Now you can sit down with your family to enjoy breakfast.

CONE COFFEE FILTERS

If you need cone filters for your coffeemaker, buy the
cheap 500-for-a-dollar round coffee filters. Fold them in
half and bend both corners an inch or so to create a cone
filter. It works great and costs a lot less than the cone-
shaped filters.

ODOR ELIMINATOR

Used coffee grinds can eliminate even the worst refrigerator odors. Simply take out the used coffee filter with the
coffee grinds in it and place it in your refrigerator in an
open container. It works better than baking soda or any
other commercial remedy. Just replace the coffee grinds
when they dry up.

CUBED EGGS

Did you know you can freeze eggs? Use an ice cube tray
and spray it with non-stick coating like Pam. Break one

egg into each compartment. Freeze. Once frozen, transfer them to a zip-type freezer bag. Do it quickly so they don't melt and stick together. Return the bag to the freezer. When you need an egg, just pop a cube from the bag. This is especially useful if you can buy eggs in bulk.

EASY DEFROST

If you do not have a frost-free freezer, do this the next time you defrost: Dry the interior walls well and then spray them with a light coating of non-stick cooking spray. This will not prevent frost from building up, but it will make it a lot easier to defrost because the ice and frost will slide off effortlessly.

TWO LOAVES, ONE LOAF PAN

If you have only one loaf pan but need to bake two loaves of bread, do this: Set the loaf pan in the middle of a 9-by-13 cake pan. The space on either side of the loaf pan is the perfect size and shape for a loaf of bread. Pour about an inch of water into the loaf pan, which creates steam during the baking process and is great for the bread.

NO MORE ICE CRYSTALS

Eliminate ice crystals on your ice cream by placing a piece of plastic wrap snuggly down on the surface of the ice cream, carefully making sure there are no pockets of air between the wrap and the ice cream. Replace the lid. Now your ice cream will be perfectly fresh down to the last bite.

EASY STORE, QUICK THAW

When hamburger is on sale buy a lot, and then put one-pound portions into freezer bags. Before closing, use your rolling pin and flatten it out. Now seal it up and stack these in the freezer. When you need a pound, it will thaw quickly because it is so thin. These flattened bags stack nicely in the freezer, too.

FILM CANISTER MEASURE

The most clever use for an empty 35mm film canister is as a spaghetti measurer. Stack uncooked spaghetti into a canister. A full canister makes spaghetti for two—no waste, no guessing. A spaghetti measurer in a fancy kitchen shop runs about $7.95.

FLAT FROZEN FOOD

If you freeze food in plastic bags, you may have a freezer filled with odd-shaped lumps of food that are difficult to organize. From now on, slip a zipped bag of food into an empty cereal box placing the whole thing into the freezer. Now the food item will freeze into a neat shape. Once frozen, slide it out of the box. Stack your freezer's contents like bricks. You'll know what you have because you'll be able to see everything, plus your freezer will operate more efficiently with less air space.

FLATWARE TIMESAVER

When loading silverware into that compartmentalized basket in the dishwasher, use one compartment for knives, one for forks and so on. Place them up and down in the compartments so they don't "nest" together. This saves a lot of time when you're putting the clean silverware away because you can just grab all of the knives, all of the forks, etc., quickly and efficiently.

FREEZER FILL UP

A completely full freezer is cheaper to run than one with big air gaps. So what do you do about gaps? Save plastic milk containers, fill with water and store in the freezer. And if the power goes out, you'll have lots of fresh cold water.

FRESH DISPOSAL

Instead of throwing citrus peels into the trash, throw them into your disposal. The oils from the peels do a great job of cleaning and refreshing the disposal.

FRESH LETTUCE

To keep lettuce fresh longer do this: Wash the lettuce, allow it to drain for a few minutes, and then place it in an airtight container or bag. But before you close it up, slip in a single paper towel. It will keep the lettuce fresh longer. It's like magic!

FRIDGE CAPS

The lightweight shower caps that hotels often leave for guests make perfect bowl covers for use in the refrigerator. They're large enough to fit most large bowls but also adjust to the smaller ones. They're easier to use than plastic wrap and reusable, too.

FROZEN RICE

Take away the hassle of cooking rice fresh every time you
want to incorporate it into your meal. You can freeze
cooked rice. So, make up a big batch; then pack it into
smaller portions and freeze. When you're ready, the exact-
sized portion you want is waiting for you.

FRUGAL LUXURY

Real vanilla sugar (for coffee drinks or to sprinkle on
cookies and other sweets) can be very expensive. Here's a
way to make a whole pound of vanilla sugar very inexpen-
sively: Place one or two vanilla beans and a pound of gran-
ulated sugar in a blender or food processor. Pulse until the
vanilla beans are invisible and the sugar is a cream-color.
This keeps very well in a covered canister.

FUN WITH FILTERS

Use coffee filters to make tea bags, coffee bags, and aroma

bags for the tub. Staple the filter in the shape you need, usually one staple will do, and then add string. It is not only practical, but fun.

HALF-PRICE SPICE

Bottled spices can be very expensive, up to $10 a bottle at some grocery stores. For a better deal, look for bulk spices packed in plastic bags. This alternative is typically priced 50 percent less than the bottles in the aisles where you find Asian, Middle Eastern, Mexican, and other ethnic foods.

KITCHEN MALLET

Kitchen mallets, used to pound meat and flatten chicken breasts are a pain to clean because the food gets stuck in the grooves of the mallet head. Try a rubber mallet (from the hardware store), and you'll find it works equally well. In fact, you can use it to whack garlic, too. A rubber mallet is easy to clean, and fits nicely in your utensil container.

LEFTOVER INVENTORY

A great way to avoid cleaning out the dreaded leftovers in the refrigerator is to keep a leftover inventory. Put a dry erase board on the front of your fridge, and each time you put a leftover in the fridge, write it down. Include the date you put it in the fridge. Then, when you use that leftover, mark it off your list. You'll save time and money.

NEWSPRINT SOLUTION

Even with the newest and most modern refrigerators, many consumers still wrap their carrots and other vegetables in newsprint, which helps preserve them longer. (Most news-papers are printed with vegetable-based inks.) Take carrots out of bag, cut off tops and wrap in newsprint as if you were wrapping flowers. Place in a plastic bag and store in the fridge. Paper absorbs moisture and keeps veggies fresh and crisp.

PROCESS WITH PLASTIC

Place a sheet of plastic wrap over the top of your food processor's bowl before applying the lid. When you remove it, all of the splatters will be confined to the bowl and the lid will be spotless.

REFRIGERATOR REDUCTION

Instead of replacing your refrigerator with one the same size, consider purchasing a mini-fridge and a chest freezer. For a lot less than the price of a refrigerator, you can get exactly what you need: lots of freezer space plus some fridge space. For small families or singles, a regular refrigerator is a waste.

SEALED PLASTIC BAGS

You can seal any plastic bag by placing a piece of aluminum foil over the end to be sealed and running a hot iron over the foil. Make sure you have foil on both sides of the plastic to be sealed so it doesn't stick to the ironing surface. No expensive sealing gadget required.

SOFT SUGAR

To keep brown sugar soft, store in a wide-mouth jar. Place a slice of bread (the heel if possible) on top of the sugar and apply the lid. Leave it on the pantry shelf and you'll have beautiful soft brown sugar all the time. Amazingly, the bread does not mold. Replace the bread each time you open the jar.

SPICY SOLUTION

Do you often end up with spices you use only once or twice before they go stale and have to be thrown out? Form a spice co-op with a friend. Now whenever either of you purchase a new spice you can share half of the container. You'll both save money and end up with a great spice collection.

TIE INTO A BOW

To keep onions fresh for a long time, cut a leg from a pair
of clean pantyhose. Slice open the toe and then tie it tightly into a bow with a piece of yarn. Now drop an onion into
the toe area and tie another yarn bow above it. Repeat until
the leg is filled with onions. Hang it to allow the onions air
space. When you need an onion, simply untie the bottom
bow. This makes the pantyhose leg reusable.

LAUNDRY

Laundry day seems to come around all too often. And while this chore can be pure drudgery and somewhat expensive—not to mention a physical drain when it comes to removing stains—there are plenty of tricks to cut costs, save time, and extend the life of your clothes. So don't fret when it's time for laundry day; tackle it head on, the cheapskate way.

Everyday Cheapskate's Greatest Tips

CONTENTS—LAUNDRY

199	Cheap Pre-Treat
199	Last Resort Clean Up
199	Cap Cleaning
200	Laundry Soap Alternative
200	Detergent Details
201	Fruit Stains
201	Inside Out
202	More from Less
202	Brighten Linens
202	Make Your Own
203	Quick Fix
203	Rust Rid
204	Salt Solution
204	Soften New Jeans
204	Softening Sponges
205	Stain Away
205	Stain Solution
206	Vinegar Softener

CHEAP PRE-TREAT

Purchase a large bottle of cheap shampoo and use as a pre-treatment for the laundry. It is especially good for the collar ring since shampoo is formulated to remove body dirt and oil.

LAST RESORT CLEAN UP

If you have a last resort stain that will not come clean with any other method, try Clorox's Clean-Up Gel as a last resort. Apply it directly to the stained area only. Launder as usual.

CAP CLEANING

Want to give new life to your baseball caps? Place them in the top rack of your dishwasher and put them through a regular wash and rinse cycle. Remove before the high-heat dry cycle. They'll come clean without losing their shape. Set on a large coffee can to air dry. Caution: Some automatic dishwasher detergents contain a small amount of bleach, which should not harm the cap. Even so, you may wish to test this method with an old cap first.

LAUNDRY SOAP ALTERNATIVE

Try this recipe in a pinch, or if your family members appear to be allergic to your laundry detergent: Add ⅛ cup baking soda and ⅛ cup Twenty Mule Team Borax as a substitute for laundry soap. You won't have any suds, but your clothes will come out clean and fresh. It's cheap, too. Depending on your particular water conditions, you may need to use slightly more of each product per load.

DETERGENT DETAILS

You may be using too much detergent when you do the laundry. Read the box to determine the amount of detergent recommended. You might find that the manufacturer's plastic cup holds almost twice the recommended amount. When the cup is filled, the box will hardly wash half the number of loads indicated in the directions. Instead, replace the cup included with your own ⅓ cup dry measuring cup. Now you'll get twice as many loads per box of detergent as before.

FRUIT STAINS

The solution of nasty fruit stains in table linens is boiling water. Everything from raspberry sauce to grape juice stains melt slowly away as the boiling water runs through them. For best results, treat as soon as possible and do not use any other method first.

INSIDE OUT

Wash your clothes inside out to keep them looking newer longer. The inside takes all of the abuse and fading caused by the agitation instead of the outside. Clothes get just as clean when washed inside out.

MORE FROM LESS

Here's a neat trick for making expensive dryer sheets last longer. Cut them lengthwise into four pieces and use one strip in each load of clothes. You won't have static cling, and a 120-count box will last about a year.

BRIGHTEN LINENS

To remove the "yellow" from old linens: Dissolve ¼ cup automatic dishwasher detergent (like powdered Cascade) in a large stainless steel pan of boiling water. (Don't try this in an aluminum pan.) Allow the items to soak for 8 hours. Rinse. Run through regular wash.

MAKE YOUR OWN

You can save money on fabric softener and dryer sheets by mixing liquid fabric softener 50/50 with water and pouring it into a spray bottle. Spray a clean, dry washcloth 6 or 7 times and toss it into the dryer with the wet clothes instead of a dryer sheet. Clothes come out very soft. A bottle of liquid fabric softener lasts a very long time employing this method.

QUICK FIX

If you're out of the house and spill something on your clothes, hit the smudge with a small amount of hand sanitizer (any brand will do). Most stains will quickly disappear. For larger stains, the help of a little water will do. Always test first in an inconspicuous place.

RUST RID

If you've tried everything you can think of to get rust out a white or lightly colored garment, don't throw the shirt away until you've tried this: Fill a large plastic bowl with cold water and add ¼ of a bottle of The Works Shower and Tub Cleaner. Put the shirt in a bowl along with a little bit of the cleaner, swish it around, rinse, and it's good as new.

SALT SOLUTION

To set the color of fabrics that may bleed or fade, dissolve one cup of salt in a bucket of enough cold water to cover the items being treated. Add the garment and mix the salt water through the fabric thoroughly. Allow to sit for at least 24 hours. The worse it bleeds, the longer you should let it sit. Wash as usual. This is not foolproof, but it's usually effective.

SOFTEN NEW JEANS

The uncomfortable stiffness of a pair of new denim jeans can be remedied by adding ½ cup salt to the wash cycle along with detergent. Your jeans will be soft and supple the first time you wear them.

SOFTENING SPONGES

Purchase a very inexpensive brand of liquid fabric softener (the cheaper the better as this suggestion doesn't work really well with the concentrates). Mix equal portions with hot water in a bucket and add cheap sponges cut into small pieces. Leave the bucket next to your dryer and squeeze out sponges to add to your dryer load. Your clothes will smell great, be soft and you can use the sponges over and over for years.

STAIN AWAY

Pre-treat perspiration stains on washable garments (even old stains), with this solution: One cup salt mixed with 2 cups water and ¼ cup liquid laundry detergent. The salt in the solution dissolves the stain. Just mix it in a spray bottle and keep it close to the washing machine. Treat the stain before washing.

STAIN SOLUTION

Instead of buying a laundry pre-treatment product, make your own. Mix equal amounts of sudsy ammonia, liquid dishwashing detergent, and water. Put this in a spray bottle. You'll have great results, especially on shirt collars.

VINEGAR SOFTENER

If you want soft, fresh-smelling clothes but don't want to pay for fabric softener, do this: Add ¼ cup of white vinegar to the last rinse of every load of laundry. It works great and is a fraction of the cost of dryer sheets or liquid fabric softener. Don't fear—your clothes won't smell like vinegar.

MONEY AND FINANCE

Who can't use a little extra money? Surely, we all can. But since it certainly does not grow on trees, it's up to us to create extra opportunities to save the money we have and to plan for a brighter economic future. Whether you need to organize your cash, set limits on its use, stretch its power, or keep an eye on its activity, the time to act is now— and always. Here are some of my favorite tips to help you curb spending, cut corners, and generally establish a positive relationship between you and your money.

CONTENTS—MONEY AND FINANCE

212	Cash Only
212	Coin Service, No Charge
213	Employee Discounts
213	Color Cash Clips
214	Credit Card Care
214	Curb the Calls
215	Waiting Period
215	Dollar Bill Bonanza
215	Expense Execution
216	Extra Paychecks
217	File For Free
217	Forgotten Money
218	Free Credit Counseling
218	Hud Refund
218	Join Up
219	Just Ask
220	One Statement, One Bill
220	Painless Contributions
220	Stamps by Mail
221	Pantry Game
222	Perks for Volunteers

222   Renew By Phone

223   Save Their Allowance

223   Secret Codes

224   Senior Discounts

224   Shipping Solution

CASH ONLY

It's a simple rule: Leave the checkbook, debit, and credit cards at home—take cash only to the store. You'll eliminate impulsive purchases and reap huge rewards. Surveys indicate a plastic-packing customer consistently spends much more than the more disciplined cash-only patron. If you see a great buy, you can always go back with more money later.

COIN SERVICE, NO CHARGE

Some banks charge a fee to accept loose coins. But if you live near a casino, you can convert your change into dollars at the cashier's cage (even mountains of pennies) for free. If you can manage to proceed directly to your vehicle without any stops to deposit cash into a machine, you'll come out a winner.

EMPLOYEE DISCOUNTS

Most colleges and universities offer their full-time employees free tuition as part of their employment benefits package. But it can get even better: Many also extend free or reduced tuition to the employee's dependent children as well.

COLOR CASH CLIPS

If you're spending only cash when you shop, knowing how much you have available in each category can be difficult when you keep all the cash together in your wallet. Use colored paper clips to organize your cash. Assign a paper clip color to each category and you can see at a glance how much you have to spend. It also might make you think twice when you're tempted to overspend and borrow from another category.

CREDIT CARD CARE

If you're afraid to carry your one and only credit card with you for fear you might use it, but you're more uncomfortable leaving it at home in case you have an emergency, there's a solution. Place the credit card into a small credit card-sized envelope and seal it. On the envelope in large red letters write "For Emergency Only." Underneath, write "Remember Your Debt." This plan should stop you from using your plastic when you shop, but you'll know if you're ever in trouble it will still be there to help.

CURB THE CALLS

Here's an effective way to reduce your long distance telephone charge: Get rid of the cordless phone and put a short cord on the phone you use. When you no longer have a cordless phone, your calls will be quicker because you won't be able to walk around and do things while you're on the phone.

WAITING PERIOD

While waiting to see if you really need an item that you've had your eye on, check the manufacturer's website to see if they are offering special coupons or rebates. When the item goes on sale, you'll save even more by using the coupon or rebate, plus you've exercised your "waiting period" option to determine that you really will use the item.

DOLLAR BILL BONANZA

Get into the habit of saving your one-dollar bills like some people save pennies. At the end of the day, remove them from your other bills and stash them away. Your stash will come in handy for a vacation or something special for the family.

EXPENSE EXECUTION

For the next two months, record all of your expenditures and organize them into categories like food, utilities, pet care, and so on. Then, concentrating on one category at a time, work to reduce the expenditures. Get on the Internet, talk to your friends, do research at the library, and do cost comparisons. Don't make the mistake of trying to cut all of your expenses at the same time. By taking one category at a time, you can make real progress that will help to keep you motivated.

EXTRA PAYCHECKS

If you get paid every two weeks, you have probably settled into living on that same amount each month. And you know that twice a year you receive a third paycheck in a month. Since you live within your means on two paychecks the other 10 months, plan to use these two "extra paychecks" to boost your savings account, fund your holiday shopping, or get a jump on a college fund.

FILE FOR FREE

The IRS has entered into a partnership agreement with more than a dozen tax software companies such as TurboTax and H&R Block to offer free Internet tax preparation and electronic filing to eligible taxpayers. So what's the catch? There is none, although there is an eligibility threshold. The IRS wants to encourage taxpayers to e-file, which saves the government a boatload of money. If your gross adjusted income is less than $28,000 or you claim the Earned Income Tax Credit, go to www.irs.gov to find a complete list of the companies offering this free service.

FORGOTTEN MONEY

Here are two painless ways to accumulate cash for the holidays: Every week hide $5 to $10 from yourself. Also, start each month with a zero balance in your checkbook (don't carry over your balance from last month). Just don't pay attention to how much you're "forgetting." You'll be amazed how quickly it adds up!

FREE CREDIT COUNSELING

Many credit unions offer counseling to members, and it's absolutely free and not reported to the credit bureaus. If you are a member of a credit union, check into the service before considering other types of credit counseling.

HUD REFUND

Housing and Urban Development (HUD) is holding literally millions of dollars of our money. If you had a HUD/FHA insured mortgage in the past, you may be eligible for a refund on part of your insurance premium or a share of the earnings. Go to www.hud.gov., type "Refunds" in the search box, and enter your name as directed.

JOIN UP

Here's a quick lesson in the difference between a credit union and a bank: Banks are for-profit corporations that benefit shareholders; credit unions are non-profit organizations formed for the benefit of its members. Generally speaking, both offer the same services. The big difference comes in what those services cost in terms of fees and interest rates on loans. You can log on to www.ncua.gov and click on "credit union data." Type in your city and state to find a list of credit unions in your area. All it takes is a quick call to see if you might qualify for membership. Note: Most credit unions are federally insured, but verify this before you decide to join one.

JUST ASK

When hiring the services of a mechanic, appliance repair, plumber, or electrician, there are few situations when it is inappropriate to kindly ask if you qualify for a discount. You will be surprised how often you'll be obliged with a 10 percent discount or more. If you don't get it, you haven't lost anything.

ONE STATEMENT, ONE BILL

Get rid of all but one credit card. Having so many credit cards can produce unnecessary stress. In fact, many cards are hazardous to your wealth. Start today with the goal to get rid of all but one.

PAINLESS CONTRIBUTIONS

Whenever you get a raise, contribute half to your 401(k). You'll still see an increase in your paycheck but you'll know your 401(k) is growing more quickly, too. Do this until you reach the maximum contribution allowed.

STAMPS BY MAIL

You can order postage stamps of any quantity and any denomination through the mail. The U.S. Postal Service even provides a postage-paid envelope in which to send the order. There is no service charge—you pay only the cost of the stamps and they always send another postage-paid envelope with the order. This can save a lot of time and eliminates the frustration if your local post office doesn't have the odd stamps you need. You can get your first form and envelope from the post office, or call and they will fax or mail it to you.

PANTRY GAME

To save time and raise cash for holiday shopping, get your family involved in playing the Pantry Game. Pretend you're stranded on a desert island and the only nourishment you have is what is presently in the pantry, refrigerator, and freezer. There's no way you will be rescued for a full week. It becomes a challenge to create meals from your precious resources. Your motivation? The grocery money that week goes into the holiday stash. See how long your family can last eating just the food you have on hand.

PERKS FOR VOLUNTEERS

By volunteering, you give back to your community but you can also save money. Volunteer at the library two hours each week and in return you might avoid late fees. You'll also get to see all the new books, and as a volunteer you're at the top of the list to borrow them. If you volunteer at your local hospital's thrift store you might have eligibility in the hospital employees' affiliated health club or other associations for discounted rates. And you'll get to see all the new thrift store merchandise. Check out the rewards for volunteering in your neighborhood.

RENEW BY PHONE

Every trip you take costs you money. However, not making a trip, such as to return library books or CDs, can cost you even more money. Save that extra trip and avoid overdue fines at the library. Most libraries will renew books over the phone.

SAVE THEIR ALLOWANCE

Here's an easy way you can begin to save for your kids' education. Many couples have a set amount to spend on lunches, commuting, and entertainment, etc., each week. Earmark the same amount each week for your kids (whether infant or older). At the end of the month, send a check to their college fund reflecting their total allowance for the month.

SECRET CODES

Most online merchants provide a place during the checkout process to enter a promotional code. Type it in and your total amount is automatically adjusted. Or you might get free shipping. Think of these codes as you would a coupon or gift certificate. You can find these codes at Web sites such as: Current Codes (www.current-codes.com); CoolSavings (www.coolsavings.com); DealCatcher (www.dealcatcher.com); EdealFinder (www.edealfinder.com); DealHunting (www.dealhunting.com); and Hot Deals Web (www.hot-dealsweb.com).

SENIOR DISCOUNTS

Many seniors live on Social Security and qualify for low-income programs with their utility companies, such as the Lifeline program with local phone companies and many long-distance carriers. Because of these programs, seniors can receive credits each month that can drastically reduce their monthly bills. If you believe you may qualify, call the service's customer service to inquire.

SHIPPING SOLUTION

Before you pay for costly overnight shipping, check the UPS normal ground delivery schedule. Often if you ship within your state or region, the regular delivery is next day. It costs about one-third of the price, usually under $5 for a one-pound parcel. And you get free tracking on www.ups.com.

ORGANIZATION AND
STORAGE

"Sorry, my place is such a mess!" **If you have to pull out that line every time you welcome friends or family into your house, it's time to act. Organization is an important aspect of any home, but so many people fail to establish a simple system to put things in their place—and keep them there. Read on to find my favorite tips for keeping everything together—from keys to safes to cords to cool storage alternatives (golf-bag tool caddy, anyone?).**

CONTENTS—ORGANIZATION AND STORAGE

230	Tape Player Tote
230	Apple Storage
231	Bag It
231	Bucket Organizer
231	Cabinet Storage Guide
232	Directory Comfort
232	Downsize for Comfort
233	Cord Corral
233	Donate to Drama
233	Drainer Do-Over
234	Earring Screen
234	Earring Holder
235	Earring Organization
235	Golf Bag Revival
236	Interim Storage
236	Key Simplify
237	Linen Closet Hang Ups
237	Plastic Bag Storage
238	Pocket those Rebates
238	Safe Keeping
239	Storage Space Solution

239   Stored Cords

239   The Law

240   Flower Power

240   The Perfect Box

TAPE PLAYER TOTE

Here's a good way to prevent your walk-around AM/FM tape player from falling off of your belt and breaking into pieces. Buy a nylon fanny pack from the dollar store and put the player in the main section with earphones and cords sticking out. Zip it up and strap it around your waist. It'll stay put even when you bend over.

APPLE STORAGE

If you have more apples than you can reasonably use in the short-term, they'll last up to six months if you store them in a dry spot between 32 to 45 degrees F. A cardboard box or Styrofoam chest in the garage, basement, or cellar can usually duplicate the conditions of an old-fashioned root cellar.

BAG IT

Hanging shoe bags are a great way to get things organized. Keep one in the broom closet for cleaning supplies and another on the back of the door to store craft and sewing supplies. You can hang one in the kids' room for all those small cars, toys, and stuffed animals. Shoe bags come in clear vinyl, plastic, and canvas, and are quite inexpensive.

BUCKET ORGANIZER

Use a large plastic bucket to store children's plastic toys. Drill several drainage holes in the bottom of the bucket and you can wash the toys in the bathtub or outdoors with the hose when the kids are finished playing.

CABINET STORAGE GUIDE

Use a digital camera to take pictures of every item that goes into each of your kitchen cabinets. Then print them in thumbnail view, one page per cabinet. Tape each handy reference guide to the inside of the cabinet doors and now your family is perfectly clear about what goes where. It's a quick guide to finding what you have stored in deep or low cabinets as well.

DIRECTORY COMFORT

If you're a military family, chances are you move a lot. Next time you move take along the local phone book to your new home. You'll find it very useful for the phone numbers and addresses of previous banks, schools, doctors, friends, etc. It's also a great resource if you want flowers delivered to the friends you left behind. You'll avoid expensive directory assistance charges.

DOWNSIZE FOR COMFORT

For many women, no matter what size purse they carry, it's completely filled. Ditch the large bag that's the size of a small state in favor of something compact. Now carry only the items you really need.

CORD CORRAL

Telephone and computer cords make home and offices unsightly. Camouflage the cords by threading them through a length of ½ inch PVC pipe attached to the wall.

DONATE TO DRAMA

Do Halloween costumes end up in boxes in your attic or garage, never to see the dark of night again? Instead of adding to the stash, get all of them out and donate them to a theatrical group or church drama department. You'll get a nice tax receipt and free up some much needed storage space, too.

DRAINER DO-OVER

Take a forgotten dish drainer that's most likely stashed under your kitchen sink and give it a new life in the office. Use it for organizing paper, pencils, pads, cards, and envelopes. It works great and will save you a few bucks from buying a desk organizer.

EARRING SCREEN

Earring organizers are all the rage in stores and boutiques. You can make your own by removing the glass and cardboard backing from a picture frame and replacing it with a piece of vinyl window screen purchased at a home improvement center and cut to the same size as the glass. Tack it in place in the same manner the glass was secured. Now you can hang your earrings through the screening so they stay organized and easy to find.

EARRING HOLDER

The next time you come across a piece of thin foam wrap (not bubble wrap) used to package fragile items, cut a strip that will fit nicely into a drawer or a compartment of your jewelry box. It makes a handy and convenient earring holder. Simply push the shank through the foam wrap and attach the earring back to the other side. The convenience of having all of your earrings secured and in the same place is well worth the couple of seconds it takes to attach them to the foam strip.

EARRING ORGANIZATION

Are you always rummaging through your jewelry box in the morning to find a matching pair of earrings? Purchase a 28-day pill organizer from a dollar store to organize your earrings. The box is clear plastic so you can easily see all of your earrings at a glance. Now they're all organized. No more rummaging!

GOLF BAG REVIVAL

An old golf bag makes a great storage caddy for all of those long-handled tools in your garage or garden storage shed. It looks cool, too.

INTERIM STORAGE

Use the plastic zippered bags that sheets and comforters come in to store clothes. Keep two or three of them in your kids' closets and toss in clothes that they outgrow. It saves time and space in their drawers and keeps the clothes clean. Once the bag is full, it's ready for the charitable collection center.

KEY SIMPLIFY

Carry only the keys you use every day like house, car, and office. Clean everything else off your key ring. If you don't recognize what a key is for, toss it. If you have keys you use occasionally, keep them on separate rings in a safe place. This will simplify your life and make your car's ignition happy, too. Heavy keys pull the ignition out of alignment increasing the odds that it will eventually fail.

LINEN CLOSET HANG UPS

If you are short on closet space but need a place to hang your tablecloths and linens, do this: Remove the bottom two shelves of a linen closet and install a closet rod. Now you can fold your tablecloth over a hanger and hang them out of the way and in their very own closet.

PLASTIC BAG STORAGE

When you finish a roll of paper towels instead of throwing away the cardboard tube use it to store your plastic grocery bags. Just keep stuffing bags into the tube until it's full, and then start on a new one. All of the tubes can be banded together with rubber bands and placed where you might need the bags. Three tubes banded together fit nicely in drawers and don't take up much room.

POCKET THOSE REBATES

Turn your kids' plastic pen and pencil holders into organizers for coupons and rebates. They have a clear front and three holes punched in the side. Buy several for different categories of coupons or rebates and place them in a small three-ring binder. Place an additional pouch in the back of your binder to hold receipts and rebate forms. Keep a supply of small envelopes, postage stamps, index cards, and pens for easy rebate-filing. The binder can also be used to keep track of family members' clothing sizes, shopping lists, to-do lists, etc. Make it something you'll never leave home without.

SAFE KEEPING

For things you would hate to lose in a fire or tornado but won't fit in a safety deposit box, do this: Put them in freezer bags and store them in your freezer. Chances are they will survive a disaster quite nicely.

STORAGE SPACE SOLUTION

If your storage space is limited and you have to stack several boxes on top of each other, make a diagram on an index card and keep it in a handy place. When you look for something, you'll know exactly where it is. Store items that you're more likely to use often toward the front with less-used items at the back.

STORED CORDS

Tangled, unorganized cords not only clutter your space but are also dangerous. Use empty paper towel and tissue rolls to store appliance cords. It keeps them neat and you can write on the roll the appliance it goes with.

THE LAW

To keep your possessions from overtaking your life and your space, declare a new personal dictum: For every new thing that comes in, something old must go out. You must obey The Law. It'll work. In fact there will be times that you'll really want to bring home something new, but the thought of getting rid of something of equal size or value will help you distinguish between a true need and a passing desire.

FLOWER POWER

Use a terra-cotta flowerpot to hold all your kitchen-cleaning tools under the sink. The terra cotta absorbs moisture, which will help to keep your tools dry and rust-free.

THE PERFECT BOX

Buy milk from Costco, two gallons to a carton, and recycle the cartons which are perfect for storing 8-by-11 sized documents and magazines. These sturdy boxes are easy to manage because they are smaller and hold less than typical storage boxes.

PETS

Pets are precious, but they're not cheap. Still, they're worth every penny. As a big part of the family, our pets deserve the best that we can give them in food, toys, healthcare, and comfort. Luckily, there are plenty of inexpensive alternatives for giving your pet healthy, safe, and fully functional toys, treats, litter options, and even medications. Here are my favorite reader tips for stretching the pet budget.

CONTENTS—PETS

244	Ant Moat
244	Anti-Odor Treatment
244	Cat Litter Mat
246	Cat Scratching Posts
246	Dog Collar
246	Do-It-Yourself Pet Meds
247	Feeding Cats
247	Litter Box Liner
248	Online Pet Meds
248	Pet Hair Removal
248	Pet Odor Treatment
249	Pills for Your Puppy
249	Bed Protection
250	That Bloated Feeling
250	Vacationing Pets

ANT MOAT

Ants are small in size but big in annoyance. If ants are getting into the pet food, put the dog or cat bowl into another shallow bowl that has water in it. Ants cannot swim.

ANTI-ODOR TREATMENT

Here's an effective cleaning solution to remove the odors resulting from pet accidents: Add 2 tablespoons of citronella oil (from the drug store) and ½ cup rubbing alcohol to 1 gallon water.

CAT LITTER MAT

Put a sisal mat or another piece of material that has a deep mat in front of the cat's litter box. Now litter won't get tracked all over the place. Once a week simply shake out the mat.

CAT SCRATCHING POSTS

If your cat prefers the furniture to the scratching post, try placing carpet samples throughout the house. For some unknown reason, many cats prefer them and will be attracted to them rather than the furniture.

DOG COLLAR

The next time one of your leather belts wears out, don't throw it away. It will make a great collar for your pet. Just cut it down to size and punch a new hole in it.

DO-IT-YOURSELF PET MEDS

Trips to the veterinarian for puppy and booster shots can be very expensive. Most reliable pet stores and grooming shops sell the medications and offer instructions so you can give the shots to your pets at home. It is easy and cheap. A typical charge for one injection at the vet office ranges from $25 to $45. The same shots from the same manufacturers purchased from grooming shops or pet stores can be more like $5 to $10 each. It is legal in most states to administer these medications to your pet. Check yours.

FEEDING CATS

Always let cat food come to room temperature before serving. Cold food straight from the refrigerator can upset a cat's stomach. And an upset cat stomach can lead to vomiting, which is never a pleasant sight—especially if it gets on your carpet.

LITTER BOX LINER

Plastic cat box liners are a waste of money. Cats tear them to shreds. Use paper grocery bags. They are tough and absorbent. Use a fresh one with each litter change.

ONLINE PET MEDS

Omaha Vaccine sells pet medications at a big discount.
Example: Heartworm pills at www.omahavaccine.com are
priced $7 less than the same product sold elsewhere.

PET HAIR REMOVAL

To remove most pet hair from furniture, especially cat hair,
put on a pair of latex gloves and rub your hands over the
furniture in one direction. Hair will clump for easy
removal.

PET ODOR TREATMENT

Diluted 50/50 with water, vinegar will take pet odors out of
carpets. Find the offending area and saturate it well (you
want to use more liquid here than the amount the pet con-
tributed). Let it set for awhile then blot all you can with a
clean white towel. Don't scrub, blot. Stand on that towel to
bring the liquid into the towel.

PILLS FOR YOUR PUPPY

Here's a quick and easy way to administer pills to sick dogs. Cut an inch or two (depending on the size of the pill) off the end of a hotdog. Scoop out the center of the hotdog and place the pill inside. Mash the scooped-out piece of hotdog back over the pill. The pill is gone in a quick swallow. Save the rest of the hotdog for the remaining daily doses.

BED PROTECTION

If your cat is one to leave "presents" on your bed, purchase a $3 clear plastic shower curtain. Spread the shower curtain on the bed after you get up and take it off just before bedtime. You can hardly see it because it is clear, and it keeps fur and other "surprises" isolated. It will prove invaluable and is easy to clean when something does happen.

THAT BLOATED FEELING

Don't let your dog eat cat food. It's not formulated to move through a dog's digestive system appropriately. Your pooch could end up in the hospital with some very serious and expensive problems.

VACATIONING PETS

Have a special ID tag for any pet that's traveling with you. Include the name and telephone number of someone who will be able to reach you while you're away. Or if your pet will be with you, make sure the tag points the way to you on vacation, not you back home.

REPAIR AND
MAINTENANCE

Maintenance costs can put a serious dent in your budget and savings—a dent that's tough to repair. And while there are certain things you definitely need an expert to handle, there are plenty of other situations in which you can make minor but meaningful repairs without the need to call in for professional support—while saving serious cash. From closet rods to roof repair, and from wallpaper tricks to paint smarts, here is a simple sampling of practical tips to help around the house.

CONTENTS—REPAIR AND MAINTENANCE

255	Closet Rod Fix
255	Goofs are Good
256	Pot Repair
256	Paint Storage
256	Hide Furniture Scratches
257	Neat Caulk
257	Split Solution
258	Wallpaper Remover
258	Freezer Paintbrush
259	Trace It with Talc
259	Perfect Pilot
260	Paint Post-Op
261	Gasket Maintenance

CLOSET ROD FIX

To fix a sagging closet rod, buy a length of ½ inch galvanized pipe and a length of ¾ inch thin-wall PVC, both the same length as your rod. You can buy these at your local home improvement center. Slip the pipe inside the PVC and slide them into the existing rod brackets. Clean the printing from the PVC with rubbing alcohol.

GOOFS ARE GOOD

Want to paint your basement floor but not spend the $100 or so that the paint store quoted? Instead ask for their oil-based goofs (paint tinted the wrong color), which work well on unsealed cement. You can usually collect five gallons for less than $25 and have more than enough for a standard size basement floor. Of course it might turn out a strange shade of gray as a result of mixing odd colors. But hey, it's a basement floor.

POT REPAIR

Don't throw out that busted terra-cotta pot. You can repair it quite easily. Moisten the breaks with water. Squeeze carpenter's glue onto the broken edges and reset the pieces. Circle the pot with strips of masking tape to hold the pieces in place. Let the bond harden.

PAINT STORAGE

Don't let those leftover portions of paint go to waist. Store partially full cans of paint upside down. The paint will form an airtight seal, extending the useful life.

HIDE FURNITURE SCRATCHES

Here's a great way to hide scratches on wood furniture: First soak the scratch with a bit of water to open the wood. Select a crayon that is as close to the right color as possible. Apply the waxy substance to the scratch; rub it in well with a soft cloth and then buff.

NEAT CAULK

If you have trouble getting the caulking around the tub or sink to look right, use this trick: Tape the tub with blue painter's tape, leaving about ¼ to ½ inch on either side of the joint for the caulking. Now squeeze the new caulk and smooth it out. Remove the tape and you have a neat and clean line and the caulk looks great. Just be sure to remove the tape before the caulk starts to set.

SPLIT SOLUTION

To prevent molding from splitting during installation, place the nails you plan to use head-end down on a solid surface and then tap the point of the nail. This blunts the point and the nail cuts through the wood rather than splitting it. This method works well on molding made from woods that have a pronounced grain such as fir, which is prone to splitting.

WALLPAPER REMOVER

Vinegar makes a great wallpaper remover. First remove all of the wallpaper you can by simply pulling it off. You'll probably get only the top layer of the paper, but that's okay. Now spray full-strength vinegar on what remains. This will begin to dissolve the glue. Once softened you'll be able to remove the rest without harsh chemicals.

FREEZER PAINTBRUSH

When tackling a painting job you may not be able to complete in one day, don't waste all of the paint in the rollers and brushes by cleaning them. Simply wrap them tightly in plastic wrap and store in the freezer. The next day, simply remove the wrap and you'll be ready to pick up right where you left off.

TRACE IT WITH TALC

Got a leaky roof, but don't know from where the leak is coming? Try this: When it's warm enough to go up into the attic, buy a container of talc powder. Wipe the underside of the roof with something like Pledge or a strong solution of Murphy's Oil Soap followed by a dusting of the talc. When you get a leak it will leave a trail through the powder and you will be able to pinpoint the entry easily. You don't want to attempt to trace a leak since it can run 20 feet from starting point to where it drips down. And don't worry that this will only increase your problem because bugs are not attracted to talc.

PERFECT PILOT

To prevent wood from splitting, professional woodworkers drill a "pilot hole" before nailing molding or floor base in place. If you can't find a bit small enough to match the nails you're using cut off the head of one of the nails with a pair of nippers. Then place it in the chuck of your power drill just as you would a regular drill bit. The nail easily cuts through the molding and makes the correct size hole for the finishing nail.

PAINT POST-OP

Most counties have Hazardous Household Material programs and collection sites where residents can drop off items that should not end up in landfills. They get all types of paint, ranging from latex, oil-based, primer, interior, exterior, and stain. Sometimes the paint dropped off at the site is brand new. Many sites have policies that allow you to take what you can use, provided you sign a waiver stating that you will use it appropriately. It's worth checking out.

GASKET MAINTENANCE

One of the first things that wears out on a refrigerator is the rubber door gasket. You can perform simple preventive maintenance by applying a very thin coat of petroleum jelly (Vaseline) to the gasket to protect it from mildew, drying and cracking. You'll improve the seal, too.

SPECIAL OCCASIONS AND HOLIDAYS

"Kodak moments" such as weddings and birthdays and holidays don't come cheap, but with some clever time- and money-saving techniques, they can be just as special, with far fewer costs. Use these time-tested readers' tips to get the best (and save the most) for all your special occasions, from cakes to flowers to gowns to invitations to party gear to all manner of holiday cheer.

CONTENTS—SPECIAL OCCASIONS AND HOLIDAYS

266	American Flags
266	Baby Shower on Ice
267	Box Building Boondoggle
267	Bridal Gown for a Day
267	Bridesmaids' Relief
268	Buy Flowers Wholesale
268	Cake Smarts
269	Christmas Book Shelf
269	Christmas Book Surprise
270	Creative Containers
270	Delete the Double Envelope
271	Gifts of Service
271	Dipe and Wipe Party
272	Drink Cooler
272	Drive-Thru Party
272	Family Recipe Book
273	Gifts of Charity
274	Honeymoon Close To Home
274	Honeymoon Off-Peak
274	Invitation Ingenuity
275	Gift List Exchange

275   Memory Lampshade
276   One-Of-A-Kind Photos
276   Origami Money
277   Potluck Reception
277   Print Your Own
278   Secret Codes
278   Special Stamps
279   Split the Shipping
279   Sap Melter
279   Think Green
280   Think Unique
280   Write It Down

AMERICAN FLAGS

The U.S. Government is an inexpensive source for high-quality American flags. Flags that have been flown over the nation's capitol can be purchased through one's senator or congressman. Flags come in either nylon or cotton and in a variety of sizes. A 3-by-5-foot nylon flag runs about $20, which includes shipping and handling. For an order form and more information, go to http://www.usflag.org/capitol.flag.html.

BABY SHOWER ON ICE

Instead of the usual baby gifts, invite the guests to bring a prepared dish, casserole, dessert, etc. completely prepared and frozen for the guest of honor's freezer. You'll be able to present the expectant parent with a freezer full of food. It's fun and inexpensive and will give your friend precious time to spend with the new baby.

BOX BUILDING BOONDOGGLE

Here's a great idea for a child's birthday party. Call an appliance store and ask for big boxes (refrigerator, stove, and dishwasher). They'll be happy to let you have whatever you need. Give the kids duct tape and tell them to make something. You'll be amazed at how this will keep their attention.

BRIDAL GOWN FOR A DAY

Rent or borrow your bridal gown. If you buy, you have to pay for it, clean it, care for it, and store it forever. It's likely you'll never open it again, opting to enjoy the pictures instead. A good rental shop includes alterations.

BRIDESMAIDS' RELIEF

No matter how hard brides try, it seems they always choose bridesmaid dresses that will never be worn again. Most of my friends had at least one in their closet, so in preparation for my own wedding I got the girls together. Each brought their collection of dresses and we mixed and matched until we found an acceptable combination. (This process helped me select my wedding colors, too.) Shopping was done, alterations were not needed, shoes were taken care of, and best of all my friends and their bank accounts were grateful.

BUY FLOWERS WHOLESALE

Beautiful flowers for your wedding don't necessarily require professional arranging. Find a talented friend to help you place them in vases, buckets or other creative containers. Warehouse discount clubs like Sam's Club and Costco offer gorgeous flowers, including roses, in growers' bunches starting at about $6 a bunch.

CAKE SMARTS

If you have a large guest list, do not buy a fancy wedding cake that feeds everyone. Buy a small, beautifully decorat-

ed cake for the photos and the cutting ceremony. Order
basic sheet cakes to serve your guests.

CHRISTMAS BOOK SHELF

Change your child's top bookshelf to 24 Christmas books,
each of a length that can be read in one night. Write the
numbers 1-24 on red and green construction paper and
tape a number to the spine of each book. Be sure to put
"1" on The Night before Christmas. Each night read that
day's story with your kids. This is a fun and inexpensive
way for the family to count down to Christmas. If you
don't have 24 books with a holiday or Christmas theme,
check used bookstores. Or ask relatives to give your kids
holiday-themed books.

CHRISTMAS BOOK SURPRISE

Instead of putting those 24 Christmas-themed books on the
shelf, wrap them as gifts and stack them in a big basket.
Let the kids open one "present" each night leading up to

Christmas. Adding an element of surprise gives anticipation to the traditional bedtime story.

CREATIVE CONTAINERS

Save containers in all shapes and sizes (shortening, chip canisters, cans with plastic lids). After Thanksgiving begin to decorate each of them using paint, decoupage, stickers, or any one of a number of things. During the early part of December bake and freeze cookies and candies. Make your own hot chocolate mix, too. As Christmas approaches, fill each container with your homemade goodies, add ribbon or bows, and deliver them to friends and family.

DELETE THE DOUBLE ENVELOPE

Save on wedding invitations by eliminating the double envelope. No one except your very proper aunt will mind, and she is going to find a problem no matter what you do.

GIFTS OF SERVICE

Many couples ask friends and family to provide services for their wedding, as their gift to the couple. Examples: Playing music during the ceremony or the reception; baking the wedding cake; doing the bride's hair and make-up. Other friends can set up and decorate the reception.

DIPE AND WIPE PARTY

If you know a couple that is expecting, throw them a Dipe and Wipe Party. Guests bring gifts of diapers and/or baby wipes. It's easy and always greatly appreciated. It's a great solution for the latest craze in baby showers. Your guest of honor won't have to buy diapers for months. And most supermarkets allow parents to exchange packages of diapers when the baby outgrows the smaller sizes. This is a nice way to take a great burden off the new parents and also serves as a great way for the father to be involved in celebrations.

DRINK COOLER

A child's wagon makes a great drink cooler for soft drinks at an outdoor party. Just load it up with ice and sodas.

DRIVE-THRU PARTY

If you find yourself with lots of little ones at a fast food restaurant, hit the drive-thru first. Just explain that you're coming inside to eat with a carload of kids and ask them to put the food on a tray at the counter. Order and pay, then park and simply walk in with the kids, grab the tray and sit down. This won't save any money, but it'll sure save your sanity.

FAMILY RECIPE BOOK

Ask all of the people in your extended family to write down two or three of their favorite recipes including one main dish and one dessert. By December have the recipes copied onto recipe cards for each family. Purchase small photo albums and insert the recipe cards into the photo slots. Give each family a recipe book of Family Favorites. This is a very personal way to give inexpensive Christmas gifts. They'll be a big hit.

GIFTS OF CHARITY

Introduce the idea of alternative gift giving to all of the adults on your gift list. Donate to a charity related to each one's special interest. For example, if your brother is an avid baseball fan, donate to a charity for low-income kids' recreation. For co-workers and other adults, make up a batch of layered soup in a jar for each recipient and include a note telling them that you have made a donation to a local soup kitchen. Wrap up a nice scarf for you mother whose favorite cause is a local shelter along with a note that you have donated a week's worth of heat to the home to make sure they have a warm and cozy holiday. Let your imagination be your guide.

HONEYMOON CLOSE TO HOME

Take a short honeymoon nearby then plan a longer vacation later after you have settled into "normal" living. It will spread the expense over a year rather than adding that cost to the wedding.

HONEYMOON OFF-PEAK

If you're planning a wedding or honeymoon think "outside the box." Winter is the off-season; Sunday through Thursday are typically off-peak days. Off-peak hours are early in the day. Book off-peak and you can cut some costs in half. January is ideal as most service providers are available and anxious for the work.

INVITATION INGENUITY

Make your own invitations. Check office supply stores for kits to use with your home computer. There are so many beautiful choices these days and, provided you proofread carefully, no one will know your secret.

GIFT LIST EXCHANGE

When it comes to exchanging gifts at holiday time, don't just draw names, draw Christmas lists! Have each member of your family write his or her name down and list some things that they would enjoy. When it comes time to draw names, all the lists go in a bowl. When you draw one, not only do you have the name of the person, you also have a list of things they would like to receive.

MEMORY LAMPSHADE

Instead of making a scrapbook for an adult son or daughter, decoupage newspaper clippings and pictures from their high school, college, and "glory days" onto an inexpensive lampshade. It will be beautiful. Hint: Apply printed text first, then pictures. Glue on braid trim in school colors around the edges.

ONE-OF-A-KIND PHOTOS

Do you love to send family pictures with your Christmas cards but hate to pay the reprint charges? Take a fresh roll of film and shoot off 24 pictures of the same pose. Kids can manage to stay still for the few minutes necessary and when you have the roll double-printed, you'll get 48 pictures for a lot less than reprinting a favorite shot. Friends and family get an updated picture and your wallet survives yet another holiday season.

ORIGAMI MONEY

Instead of sending Gift Cards (they can be troublesome and offer the recipient only one store choice), give the real thing—$5, $10, and $20 bills folded into fun shapes. Then enclose them with a note in an envelope. Get a book from the library or search on the Internet to find instructions for how to fold money into frogs, cranes, trees, even a ring. The recipients can enjoy them for a few days, then unfold and spend as they like. Cash never expires the way some gift cards do. And it's good anywhere.

POTLUCK RECEPTION

If you're getting married, but don't really need gifts, ask your guests to bring a potluck dish to the wedding reception in lieu of a gift. Is there anything better than potluck food? And instead of wedding cards, request that your guests bring the recipe for the dish and sign the recipe card. For the right situation, this can be a great, simple, and delicious change of wedding protocol.

PRINT YOUR OWN

Go to www.freeprint.com where you'll find useful Christmas and Hanukkah items you can print for only the cost of paper and ink. Just use the print commands in your web browser to make beautiful gift tags, greeting cards, calendars, signs, and pictures.

SECRET CODES

Instead of purchasing nametags, use color-coded stars or stickers to identify to whom the gifts under the tree are for. Keep the code a secret until Christmas morning. Saves time and money and adds to the excitement and suspense. Especially effective for the overly curious spouse or child.

SPECIAL STAMPS

Buy your holiday postage from a coin and stamp dealer that sells new, uncancelled stamps below their face value. Many are older stamps in small denominations but are not worth more than their face value to collectors. To get rid of them, dealers often negotiate a price below the face value. Bonus: Your recipients get really cool looking vintage mail. Check the Yellow Pages or online for a dealer.

SPLIT THE SHIPPING

Save money when Christmas shopping online or by mail order. Combine your order with a friend's and split the shipping and handling fees.

SAP MELTER

If you collect pine cones to use for crafts and holiday decorations, some might be so sticky with sap there's no way you can use them. Here's a great solution: Put them on a cookie sheet and into a *300*° F oven for 10 minutes. The whole house will smell piney fresh right away, and any sap that doesn't melt away hardens in just a few minutes as they cool.

THINK GREEN

Salad bar wedding receptions (dessert bars, too) are becoming more popular because they're cost-effective and people love them. You can include a salad bar, fruit salads, pasta salads and so on. If you do a lot of the work yourselves, you'll save even more.

THINK UNIQUE

Call the Historical Building Preservation Society in your town to learn which facilities are for rent. In some cases, you can rent a beautiful historic home complete with grounds for a very reasonable price. Many locations come fully furnished including tables and chairs for their guests. Or consider an arboretum. The grounds are always so beautiful there's no need for any additional décor or flowers other than bouquets and boutonnières.

WRITE IT DOWN

So that you won't get confused and over-buy, create a spreadsheet to track what you have purchased and what you have remaining to buy for the holidays. List the person, planned expense, actual expense, item purchased, and amount over/under the plan. This will help a lot!

TRAVEL AND ENTERTAINMENT

There's no reason why your travel and entertainment plans need to be put on the shelf just because your overall budget is tight. And when you do travel, it's best to take steps to make your trip as comfortable as can be. Here are some great ways to find cheap travel and to make all your adventures hassle-free. After all, what are work and savings good for if you can't enjoy the fruits of your labor now and again?

CONTENTS—TRAVEL AND ENTERTAIMENT

286	Camera Bag
286	Telltale Sign
287	Cheap Entertainment
287	Campus Bargains
288	Car Organizer
288	Carry on Consideration
288	Sand Free Radio
289	Passport Photos
289	Feeless Fares
290	Disappearing Ink
290	Give and Take
291	Home Time
291	Lost Passport
292	Luggage Trick
292	Packing List
292	Packing Plastic
293	Plant Vacation Care
293	Put a Lid on It
294	Photocopies Just In Case
294	Save on Room Rates
294	Shampoo Your Clothes

295	Single Bag
295	Stains on the Road
295	Take the Tape
296	Test the Weight
296	Travel Iron
297	Traveling Make-Up Remover
297	Vacation Values
297	Floating Keys

CAMERA BAG

Fill a small fabric bag with dried beans or rice and keep it in your camera bag. When you want to take a time-exposure shot and need to hold the camera very still, simply set the bean bag on a steady surface, place the camera on the bag, line up the shot and shoot. The camera stays perfectly still because it is securely cradled on the beanbag. This is also a perfect solution for when you want to get into the photo, too. Just securely position the camera on the beanbag, set the timer, and run like crazy.

TELLTALE SIGN

Before you leave on a trip, place a few ice cubes into a small container and set it in the freezer. When you get home take a look at it. If the cubes are still intact, you'll know there was no power outage while you were way. If they've melted and then refrozen into a different shape, you'll know the power went out for an extended period and that the food in the freezer may no longer be safe to eat.

CHEAP ENTERTAINMENT

Be on the lookout for church or social hall dinners and festivals. Many churches hold dinners as fundraisers and social clubs. For example, the VFW and Knights of Columbus frequently put on pancake breakfasts. These meals are usually quite delicious, very reasonably priced, and provide wonderful opportunities to meet new people and support good causes. Can't get that from a drive-thru.

CAMPUS BARGAINS

College coffee shops are very popular across America, especially for the general public. You can buy good coffee and lattes for about a third of the cost of other coffee shops. The food on many campuses is good and very reasonable, and you don't have to be alumni or a student to patronize. And campus bookstores have great sales, too!

Everyday Cheapskate's Greatest Tips

CAR ORGANIZER

A pocket shoe bag hung over the back of the front seat can
hold small toys, crayons, and other loose items in the car.

CARRY ON CONSIDERATION

It may sound like mission impossible but if you learn to
travel light with only your carry-on you will save a tremen-
dous amount of time and money. You can ride the bus
instead of hiring a cab. You won't have to tip porters to
carry all your suitcases. And if your flight is over booked,
you can volunteer to get bumped (you'll get a voucher for
a free ticket), and not worry about whether you will ever
catch up with your checked luggage.

SAND FREE RADIO

When you go to the beach, lake, river, or pool, carry the
radio in a clear plastic zipper-type bag. You can operate

it without ever opening the bag. It will stay sand-free and totally dry.

PASSPORT PHOTOS

The U.S. passport application requires two identical full-face photographs, with the face 1 to $1\frac{1}{2}$ inches high. It's simple to take that photo yourself, which beats spending $10 or more at a studio for a photo that doesn't even look like you. Take about seven shots of each of your family members. Knowing the finished print would be 4 by 6 inches, focus on the face and position yourself so the face takes up one-quarter of the frame. Get double prints, pick out the best shot and save a bundle.

FEELESS FARES

To get the least expensive plane fare, go to a couple of the popular travel sites like Expedia, Orbitz, Travelocity, etc., and find the cheapest option there. Then call the airline directly. Give the agent the fight numbers and wait for them to quote you the price. They'll most likely quote either the Internet fare or less. You won't have to pay the travel site's fee to buy the tickets online, which should be a savings of at least $5 a ticket.

DISAPPEARING INK

A disappearing-ink marking pen, available at any fabric or quilt store, is great for marking maps. In a day or so, your marks will fade and your map is all ready for the next trip.

GIVE AND TAKE

At the start of a trip, give each child a roll of dimes or quarters. If they ask, "How much farther?" "Are we there yet?" etc., they forfeit a dime. Let them keep what's left.

HOME TIME

If you take medications, take an extra watch and keep it always set on home time. You'll never have to wonder when to take your medicine.

LOST PASSPORT

You can ease the pain of losing your passport while traveling abroad if you simply take an extra passport photo with you. Keep it in a safe yet separate place from your passport, along with your passport number, and the date of issue. Now all you have to do is take the photo and numbers to the closest U.S. Embassy. It should take hours, not days to get a replacement. (It is illegal to photocopy a passport.)

LUGGAGE TRICK

When traveling by air with a companion, be sure each checked piece of luggage has a change of clothing and some toiletries for the other person. That way if a bag gets lost or is delayed (chances are at least one will show up), you'll both have at least one change of clothing.

PACKING LIST

Toss the checked-off packing list you used to prepare for the trip into your suitcase. Use it to re-check when gathering everything at the end of your stay.

PACKING PLASTIC

Plastic dry-cleaning bags are great for packing clothes when you travel. Just leave the garment in the bag and fold or roll it. When you unpack you'll be amazed that there are no wrinkles! Caution: Left on clothes over time, the plastic contributes to mildew and discoloration, so do not store your clothes in dry-cleaning bags.

PLANT VACATION CARE

Before taking off for your summer vacation, thoroughly soak and feed your houseplants and then cluster them together in an empty bathtub or child's swimming pool. Set in a sunny location or provide your plants with artificial lighting while you are away. Cover them completely with a lightweight tent of clear plastic and tightly seal it with tape on all sides. No more water necessary. This will work for up to two weeks.

PUT A LID ON IT

To make sure that bottles of shampoo, lotions and makeup in your suitcase don't leak all over your clothes, put a bit of cotton inside each bottle cap before closing the container.

PHOTOCOPIES JUST IN CASE

Before you leave on vacation, make two photocopies of everything in your wallet both front and back (credit card, driver's license, medical insurance card, etc.). Put one copy inside your luggage and leave the other at home. If you should lose your wallet, you'll have all the information you need to quickly report and replace.

SAVE ON ROOM RATES

Always call the hotel desk instead of the central 800 reservation number to get the best deals. Ask about weekend rates, holiday, and seasonal specials, or discounts for affiliations you might have such as the Automobile Club of America.

SHAMPOO YOUR CLOTHES

Don't bother packing laundry detergent. The shampoo you bring or you find in your hotel room is great for washing blouses and underwear. Caution: Shampoos formulated for oily hair are more alkaline and should not be used on delicate fabrics like silk, as they can cause fading.

SINGLE BAG

If an overnight stop is on your car trip itinerary, pack a small bag with one change of clothes for each family member and basic toiletries. Instead of unpacking the whole car, everything you'll need for the night is in just one bag.

STAINS ON THE ROAD

Pack a laundry stain pretreatment in your luggage and use it on stains before they can set. This way, stains will wash out easily once you're home and get to the laundry.

TAKE THE TAPE

When traveling, always take a roll of cellophane tape. It

removes lint, seals bottles and even temporarily mends cuffs and hems. Duct tape works well too, particularly where stronger mending is needed like shoe repair or suitcase patches.

TEST THE WEIGHT

After packing for a trip and just before leaving the house, pick up your bag and carry it around for a full five minutes. If you're out of breath, it's too heavy. Eliminate what you can or pack two smaller, lighter-weight bags instead of a single heavy bag.

TRAVEL IRON

A hair dryer can double as a travel iron. Dampen the creased garment and spread it on a flat surface. Set the dryer on warm, and hold it in one hand while smoothing the item with the other.

TRAVELING MAKE-UP REMOVER

Instead of packing a bottle of baby oil (used to remove makeup), saturate cotton balls with the oil and drop them into a zip-type plastic bag. No mess, no spills, no storage problems.

VACATION VALUES

Before you book your next vacation, find out when your local public television station is having a pledge drive. There is almost always a travel package to bid on. The winning bid is generally a fraction of the value of the trip.

FLOATING KEYS

Just to be on the safe side, tie a couple of corks to your key ring when you go boating. Finding them on the surface of the water is much easier than the bottom, which could be impossible.

YARD AND GARDEN

The yard and garden are great places to dig into the dirt with a multitude of projects, or to relax and simply enjoy a quiet moment. To make the most of your experience in the great outdoors, you'll want to keep your plants and flowers healthy every day while keeping pests and high costs away. Here are my hand-picked tips that offer simple and smart tricks for keeping your outdoor areas in great shape without digging too deeply into your wallet.

Everyday Cheapskate's Greatest Tips

CONTENTS—YARD AND GARDEN

302   Aerate the Lawn

302   Alcohol Kills

302   Ant Repellant

303   Aquarium Recycle

303   Better Blossoming Bulbs

304   Build Soil with Ashes

304   Carpet Mulch

304   Cheap Fertilizer

305   Cheaper Mower

305   Coffee Grounds Collection

306   Comfy Knee Pad

306   Fels Naptha Kills Bugs

307   Free Flowers

307   Garden Cart

308   Germination Tests

308   Grass Clippings

308   Homely but Useful

309   Homemade Lawn Food

309   Lawn Snack

310   Increase Acidity

310   Keep Cats Away With Ammonia

310 Lubricate the Garden Hose
311 Rodent Deterrent
311 Newspaper Weed Control
311 Pantyhose Tie-Ups
312 Pepper is a Cat Deterrent
312 Plant Flowers
313 Plant Protectors
313 Plant with Purpose
314 Promote New Growth
314 Rust-Free Tools
315 Safe Pest Control
315 Soap on a Spigot
315 Sprinkler Stand
316 Trial Garden
316 Vinegar Kills
316 Easy Spacing
317 Nix Ants with Nutrasweet
317 Salty Solution

AERATE THE LAWN

Wear golf shoes or other spiked athletic shoes while mowing the lawn. You will aerate the grass roots with each step, which allows much needed oxygen and water to nourish the lawn.

ALCOHOL KILLS

Rubbing alcohol kills roaches faster than commercial insecticides. Just keep it in a spray bottle and a couple of squirts will do the trick. Label the spray bottle clearly and store well out of the reach of children.

ANT REPELLANT

Rubbing alcohol works great to get rid of ants. Clean the surface where ants appear, allow it to dry, then spray rubbing alcohol but do not rinse. If you do this on your counter, just buff off the white residue with a soft cloth or paper towel. The rubbing alcohol "erases" the ant tracks, and it dehydrates and kills any ants that come in contact with it.

AQUARIUM RECYCLE

Here's a great use for an old fish aquarium, lid, and light (even if it leaks): Use it for a seed-starting greenhouse. Stack several layers of scrap wood in the bottom of the tank to get the seed-starting flats close to the fluorescent lights. With the lid closed, the moisture in the soil will keep the space humid. As the seeds germinate and the sprouts begin to grow take pieces of wood away board by board to accommodate their height.

BETTER BLOSSOMING BULBS

In the fall, resist the urge to remove the foliage after your bulbs have finished blooming. Let the leaves wither naturally so that the bulb has lots of time to manufacture nutrients and fatten up for next year. Now your bulbs will perform as true perennials.

BUILD SOIL WITH ASHES

Spread wood ash from your winter fires onto the garden beds. Also known as potash, it will gradually build the soil, adding potassium as well as 32 trace minerals. And it's free!

CARPET MULCH

If the area you choose for your vegetable garden is covered with millions of tiny weeds, don't despair. Preparation of the soil may appear to be overwhelming, but it's not. Cover the area with an old piece of carpeting, leaving the weeds and all. Make a 3-inch cross cut for each seedling you will plant. Next, lift each cut, dig a hole beneath and set the plants. You'll have a very colorful garden, vigorous plant growth and gorgeous easy-to-harvest vegetables.

CHEAP FERTILIZER

Add 2 teaspoons plain household ammonia to 1 gallon

water. Allow to sit in an open container (and out of the reach of kids looking for a drink) for a full 24 hours. Use on plants instead of commercial fertilizer. Caution: More is not better. If you use more ammonia, it will be too strong and you will burn your plants.

CHEAPER MOWER

Lawn mower repair shops offer great deals in used, recon-ditioned lawn mowers. You can purchase a beautiful, like-new self-propelled mower, in tiptop shape, with all the lat-est features for less than a new, basic model offered by a discount warehouse store. As a bonus, you can expect a good mower shop to stand behind what it sells with the ability to repair on the spot.

COFFEE GROUNDS COLLECTION

If you don't drink coffee, but are always searching for ways to acquire coffee grounds for your compost, just pro-vide containers to the cafe in your office building.

Employees are usually happy to dump the grounds into your containers and that will give you plenty of grounds to enrich your compost.

COMFY KNEE PAD

To make a cheap and comfortable kneeling pad, purchase two 8-foot lengths of foam plastic and ¾ inch water pipe insulation for about $1.20 each. Cut each length of insulation into four pieces, making eight pieces. Use duct tape and tape the pieces together side by side (not stacked). This is enough for a kneeling pad approximately 18-by-14-inches. It is not only cheap but very comfortable, especially when working on cold or wet concrete floors because the insulation keeps your knees warm.

FELS NAPTHA KILLS BUGS

The best thing to spray flowers and veggies to stop a bug invasion is grated Fels Naptha bar soap mixed together with water in a spray bottle. Shake vigorously and spray.

It's non-toxic, and it works well. Find Fels Naptha bar soap in the laundry aisle of your grocery store, or online at www.soapsgonebuy.com

FREE FLOWERS

Perennial flowers are routinely pulled from flower beds at entrances to large business parks and prestigious housing developments, and are generally thrown in the trash. Ask the workers if you can have some of the flowers. Chances are they'll give you all that you can take. It's a lot of work at the end of the season to get them back into the ground, but when the flowers start blooming all over your yard it's worth it. And it's all for free.

GARDEN CART

Use a child's plastic snow sled as an off-season garden cart. It glides easily over the grass for cleanup chores and is especially handy when it's time to lift and divide clumps of perennials.

GERMINATION TESTS

Test old seeds to see if they're worth planting: Place 10 seeds on a dampened paper towel. Cover with plastic to keep them moist. Check seeds after the germination time listed on the package has passed. If some but not all seeds germinate you can still use the packet. Just be sure to sow the seeds more heavily than usual.

GRASS CLIPPINGS

Place grass clippings around plants to repel weeds. The clippings also retain moisture and are a good source of nutrients.

HOMELY BUT USEFUL

Don't throw out that bleach bottle with a handle. When it's empty, just rinse it thoroughly, trim the bottom at an angle and you've got a heavy-duty garden scoop.

HOMEMADE LAWN FOOD

Mix the following in a large container: 1 cup Epsom salts, 1 cup antiseptic mouthwash, 1 cup liquid dish soap, 1 cup ammonia, 1 can of beer. Fill a hose-end sprayer jar, attach to the hose with the dial set so this recipe mixes with 20 gallons of water. Give your lawn a generous dose. Yum.

LAWN SNACK

Try this on your lawn every three weeks during the summer: Mix together 1 can of beer, 1 cup baby shampoo, and household ammonia. Pour the beer and shampoo into a hose-end sprayer jar. Fill the jar with ammonia and apply according to the hose-end sprayer instructions for coverage at 2000 square feet. Every third snack, add ½ cup clear corn syrup or molasses to the mixture. You're going to have very happy grass.

INCREASE ACIDITY

Drench wet soil with full strength white vinegar (or a 50/50 vinegar and water solution on dry soil) to increase the acidity of the soil for plants like azaleas and gardenias.

KEEP CATS AWAY WITH AMMONIA

Sink small open containers (baby food jars are good) into the soil up to the rim throughout the garden and fill with household ammonia. Cats hate the smell of ammonia.

LUBRICATE THE GARDEN HOSE

To prevent the end of a hose from becoming attached to the spigot so tightly that you cannot easily remove it without the aid of tools, rub a light coating of petroleum jelly (Vaseline) on the hose end.

RODENT DETERRENT

If chipmunks and rodents are dining on your newly planted bulbs, discourage them by sprinkling a pinch of moth crystals over each bulb as you plant it. The crystals will last long enough to deter hungry rodents and then evaporate into the soil. By winter, the soil will have compacted around the bulbs so rodents won't dig for them.

NEWSPAPER WEED CONTROL

Newspaper is cheap and works beautifully for controlling weeds. Cover the area where you plan to cultivate seeds or plants with 10 layers of newspaper, then spread mulch or compost over the top. To plant, simply poke a hole in the paper and insert the seed or seedling.

PANTYHOSE TIE-UPS

Save your old pantyhose to use in your garden. Cut them in long strips and then use them to tie tomato plants to the stakes or tomato cages. The strips are great for tying other vegetables (string beans, cucumbers, viney plants) to the fences. Nylons are better than string because they stretch and don't cut off the plants' circulation. And they blend in visually as well.

PEPPER IS A CAT DETERRENT

Sprinkle the garden with ground black pepper. Purchase it in bulk at a warehouse club or bulk grocer and apply liberally to affected area. It won't harm the cats, but simply irritates their paws so they'll go somewhere else to dig.

PLANT FLOWERS

Marigolds have a pungent odor that repels cats and other bugs and animals. Plant them among your vegetable and flower gardens.

PLANT PROTECTORS

The rolls from your toilet tissue make great planting "col-lars" for tomato and other small seedlings. Dig a hole, drop in a handful of crushed eggshells (calcium), and two small pieces of banana peel (potassium). Plant the seedling then slip the tube over the top to protect the plant from wind while it grows and takes root. Push about ⅓ of the tube into the soil to give it stability.

PLANT WITH PURPOSE

Plant deciduous trees (the type that lose their leaves in winter) on the south side of your house. They will provide summer shade without blocking winter sun. Plant ever-greens on the north to shield your home from cold winter winds.

PROMOTE NEW GROWTH

To guarantee the healthiest plants in town, when planting trees, shrubs, and evergreens, scatter 10 unused match heads and 1 cup of Epsom salts in the planting hole. This promotes new growth and helps strengthen stems and roots.

RUST-FREE TOOLS

Put enough play sand in a cheap, galvanized bucket to fill it three-quarters of the way to the top. Add enough motor oil so you can just barely see the color, leaving it mostly sand. When you are finished gardening for the day, or for the season, put your tools in the bucket blades down and they will be clean, oiled, rust-free, and ready to go for your next gardening adventure.

SAFE PEST CONTROL

Don't battle bugs on your tomatoes and other garden plants anymore. Treat them with rubbing alcohol. Spray it directly on the plants. It kills mildew, aphid, whitefly, scale, and many other pests and is safe to use on produce.

SOAP ON A SPIGOT

Put a bar of soap in the toe of a pantyhose leg, tie a knot over it, and tie the other end to an outdoor spigot. Gardeners can easily wash up after working.

SPRINKLER STAND

Turn your spade into an extra pair of hands. Whenever you need a direct flow of water onto a portion of your garden, simply stick the spade into the soil and nestle your hose into the V-shaped notch where the handle begins.

TRIAL GARDEN

Make a temporary garden out of a plastic kiddy pool. It's just the right size for beginners and children because it can be placed in the best light and can be disassembled and put away for the winter.

VINEGAR KILLS

Vinegar as a weed killer is very effective. And if you can spray your vinegar on those pesky ants while it's as if you've hit the jackpot!

EASY SPACING

Mark the handles of your gardening tools with 1-inch increments. You will no longer need a ruler when planting or spacing plants, shrubs, or flowers.

NIX ANTS WITH NUTRASWEET

Next time there's an invasion of ants, spread a single packet of Nutrasweet (or other sweetener that contains aspartame) over part of the trail. One treatment should get rid of all the ants in less than a day. Try it and see. Then reconsider whether you want to use the stuff in your drinks.

SALTY SOLUTION

In the hot and sticky days of summer, ants seem to appear from nowhere to invade a home. To keep them away, spread a thin line of salt across the places they want to enter. Ants will not cross a line of salt.

A NOTE FROM MARY HUNT

More Tips!If you feel a certain sadness because you've come to the end of this book, don't despair. You can find so many more tips and so much more in my daily newspaper column, *Everyday Cheapskate*. To receive information on getting *Everyday Cheapskate* in your paper, e-mail the Sales Manager at United Media, *sales@unitedmedia.com*.

In the meantime, please consider this your personal invitation to visit my website, *www.cheapskatemonthly.com*, home of my monthly subscription newsletter, *The Cheapskate Monthly*, and other great money-saving advice.

I would love to hear from you! You can write to me: *cheapskate@unitedmedia.com*.